Physical Science Grade 4

S0-BAQ-206

Table of Contents

Physical Science Grade 4
Introduction

We wake up in a new world every day. Our lives are caught in a whirlwind of change. New wonders are discovered almost daily. Technology is carrying us headlong into the 21st century. How will our children keep pace? We must provide them with the tools necessary to go forth into the future. Those tools can be found in a sound science education. One guidepost to a good foundation in science is the National Science Education Standards. This book adheres to these standards.

Young children are interested by almost everything around them. They constantly ask questions about how and why things work. They should be encouraged to observe their world, the things in it, and how things interact. They should take note of the properties of the Earth and its materials, distinguish one material from another, and then try to develop their own explanation of why things are the way they are. A basic understanding of science boosts students' understanding of the world around them.

As children learn more about their world, they should be encouraged to notice the world around them, such as the color of the sky, the bark of a dog, a rainbow after it rains, the movement of a bicycle.

Organization
Physical Science serves as a handy companion to the regular science curriculum. It is broken into three units: Sound Off!; Let It Shine!; and A Simple Force. Each unit contains concise background information on the unit's topics, as well as exercises and activities to reinforce students' knowledge and understanding of basic principles of science and the world around them.

- **Sound Off!:** Students learn that sound is a form of energy made when objects vibrate. They will discover how sound travels and why we can hear. Students have the opportunity to make musical instruments as they explore the relationship of music and sound. Finally, students learn the uses of sound energy in the field of communication and geography.

- **Let It Shine!:** Students begin to understand the basic concepts and characteristics of light through numerous experiments. They explore movement, reflection, refraction through a variety of mediums, especially mirrors and glass. Moreover, they discover how their eyes work and the reasons we view the world in color.

- **A Simple Force:** This unit gives information on force and friction. Students also focus on the six kinds of simple machines. They learn how pulleys, levers, inclined planes, screws, wedges, and wheels and axles make work easier.

This book contains three types of pages:
- Concise background information is provided for each unit. These pages are intended for the teacher's use or for helpers to read to the class.
- Exercises are included for use as tests or practice for the students. These pages are meant to be reproduced.
- Activity pages list the materials and steps necessary for students to complete a project. Questions for students to answer are also included on these pages as a type of performance assessment. As much as possible, these activities include most of the multiple intelligences so students can use their strengths to achieve a well-balanced learning style. These pages are also meant for reproduction for use by students.

Use

Physical Science is designed for independent use by students who have been introduced to the skills and concepts described. This book is meant to supplement the regular science curriculum; it is not meant to replace it. Copies of the activities can be given to individuals, pairs of students, or small groups for completion. They may also be used as a center activity. If students are familiar with the content, the worksheets may also be used as homework.

To begin, determine the implementation that fits your students' needs and your classroom structure. The following plan suggests a format for this implementation.

1. Explain the purpose of the worksheets to your students. Let them know that these activities will be fun as well as helpful.
2. Review the mechanics of how you want the students to work with the activities. Do you want them to work in groups? Are the activities for homework?
3. Decide how you would like to use the assessments. They can be given before and after a unit to determine progress, or only after a unit to assess how well the concepts have been learned. Determine whether you will send the tests home or keep them in students' portfolios.
4. Introduce students to the process and the purpose of the activities. Go over the directions. Work with children when they have difficulty. Work only a few pages at a time to avoid pressure.
5. Do a practice activity together.

The Scientific Method

Students can be more productive if they have a simple procedure to use in their science work. The scientific method is such a procedure. It is detailed here, and a reproducible page for students is included on page 7.

1. PROBLEM: Identify a problem or question to investigate.
2. HYPOTHESIS: Tell what you think will be the result of your investigation or activity.
3. EXPERIMENTATION: Perform the investigation or activity.
4. OBSERVATION: Make observations, and take notes about what you observe.
5. CONCLUSION: Draw conclusions from what you have observed.
6. COMPARISON: Does your conclusion agree with your hypothesis? If so, you have shown that your hypothesis was correct. If not, you need to change your hypothesis.
7. PRESENTATION: Prepare a presentation or report to share your findings.
8. RESOURCES: Include a list of resources used. Students need to give credit to people or books they used to help them with their work.

Hands-On Experience

An understanding of science is best promoted by hands-on experience. *Physical Science* provides a wide variety of activities for students to do. But students also need real-life exposure to their world. Playgrounds, parks, and vacant lots are handy study sites to observe many of nature's forces.

It is essential that students be given sufficient concrete examples of scientific concepts. Appropriate manipulatives can be bought or made from common everyday objects. Most of the activity pages can be completed with materials easily accessible to the students. Manipulatives that can be used to reinforce scientific skills are recommended on several of the activity pages.

Science Fair

Knowledge without application is wasted effort. Students should be encouraged to participate in their school science fair. To help facilitate this, each unit in *Physical Science* ends with a page of science fair ideas and projects. Also, on page 8 is a chart that will help students to organize their science fair work.

To help students develop a viable project, you might consider these guidelines:

- Decide whether to do individual or group projects.
- Help students choose a topic that interests them and that is manageable. Make sure a project is appropriate for a student's grade level and ability. Otherwise, that student might become frustrated. This does not mean that you should discourage a student's scientific curiosity. However, some projects are just not appropriate. Be sure, too, that you are familiar with the school's science fair guidelines. Some schools, for example, do not allow glass or any electrical or flammable projects. An exhibit also is usually restricted to three or four feet of table space.
- Encourage students to develop questions and to talk about their questions in class.
- Help students to decide on one question or problem.
- Help students to design a logical process for developing the project. Stress that the acquisition of materials is an important part of the project. Some projects also require strict schedules, so students must be willing and able to carry through with the process.

- Remind students that the scientific method will help them to organize their thoughts and activities. Students should keep track of their resources used, whether they are people or print materials. Encourage students to use the Internet to do research on their project.

Additional Notes

- Parent Communication: Send the Letter to Parents home with students so that parents will know what to expect and how they can best help their child.
- Bulletin Board: Display completed work to show student progress.
- Portfolios: You may want your students to maintain a portfolio of their completed exercises and activities or of newspaper articles about current events in science. This portfolio can help you in performance assessment.
- Assessments: There are Assessments for each unit at the beginning of the book. You can use the tests as diagnostic tools by administering them before children begin the activities. After children have completed each unit, let them retake the unit test to see the progress they have made.
- Center Activities: Use the worksheets as a center activity to give students the opportunity to work cooperatively.
- Have fun: Working with these activities can be fun as well as meaningful for you and your students.

Physical Science Grade 4
Curriculum Correlation

Language Arts	66, 108
Math	28, 47, 48, 49, 50,53, 65, 67, 69, 70, 73, 74, 77, 78, 79, 80, 81, 82, 92, 96, 109, 110, 112, 115, 116, 121, 122, 127, 128, 133, 135, 136, 137, 138
Social Studies	19, 23, 45, 46, 47, 48, 49, 51, 52, 69, 70, 97, 98, 99, 101, 111, 112, 117, 123, 124
Health/PE	39, 53, 73, 74, 87, 89, 90, 101, 102, 107, 110, 118, 131
Music/Art	20, 31, 32, 33, 34, 35, 36, 37, 38, 41, 99, 100, 101

FOSS Curriculum Correlation

The Full Option Science System™ (FOSS) was developed at the University of California at Berkeley. It is a coordinated science curriculum organized into four categories: Life Science; Physical Science; Earth Science; and Scientific Reasoning and Technology. Under each category are various modules that span two grade levels. The modules for this grade level are highlighted in the chart below.

Sound	15-18, 19, 20, 21-22, 23, 24, 25, 26, 27, 28, 29-30, 31-32, 33-34, 35, 36, 37, 38, 39, 40, 41-42, 43-44, 45, 46, 47, 48, 49-50, 51-52, 53, 54
Magnetism & Electricity	15, 18, 54

Physical Science 4, SV 3763-1

Dear Parent,

During this school year, our class will be using an activity book to reinforce the science skills we are learning. By working together, we can be sure that your child not only masters these science skills but also becomes confident in his or her abilities.

From time to time, I may send home activity sheets. To help your child, please consider the following suggestions:

- Provide a quiet place to work.
- Go over the directions together.
- Help your child to obtain any materials that might be needed.
- Encourage your child to do his or her best.
- Check the activity when it is complete.
- Discuss the basic science ideas associated with the activity.

Help your child to maintain a positive attitude about the activities. Let your child know that each lesson provides an opportunity to have fun and to learn more about the world around us. Above all, enjoy this time you spend with your child. As your child's science skills develop, he or she will appreciate your support.

Thank you for your help.

Cordially,

The Scientific Method

Did you know you think and act like a scientist? You can prove it by following these steps when you have a problem. These steps are called the scientific method.

1. Problem: Identify a problem or question to investigate.

_____

_____

_____

2. Hypothesis: Tell what you think will be the result of your investigation or activity.

_____

_____

_____

3. Experimentation: Perform the investigation or activity.

_____

_____

4. Observation: Make observations, and take notes about what you observe.

_____

_____

_____

5. Conclusion: Draw conclusions from what you have observed.

_____

_____

_____

6. Comparison: Does your conclusion agree with your hypothesis? If so, you have shown that your hypothesis was correct. If not, you need to change your hypothesis.

_____

7. Presentation: Prepare a presentation or report to share your findings.

_____

8. Resources: Include a list of resources used. You need to give credit to people or books you used to help you with your work.

_____

_____

_____

The Science Fair

The science fair at your school is a good place to show your science skills and knowledge. Science fair projects can be several different types. You can do a demonstration, make a model, present a collection, or perform an experiment. You need to think about your project carefully so that it will show your best work. Use the scientific method to help you to organize your project. Here are some other things to consider:

Project Title _____

Working Plan	Date Due	Date Completed	Teacher Initials
1. Select topic			
2. Explore resources			
3. Start notebook			
4. Form hypothesis			
5. Find materials			
6. Investigate			
7. Prepare results			
8. Prepare summary			
9. Plan your display			
10. Construct your display			
11. Complete notebook			
12. Prepare for judging			

Write a brief paragraph describing the hypothesis, materials, and procedures you will include in your exhibit.

Be sure to plan your project carefully. Get all the materials and resources you need beforehand. Also, a good presentation should have plenty of visual aids, so use pictures, graphs, charts, and other things to make your project easier to understand.

Be sure to follow all the rules for your school science fair. Also, be prepared for the judging part. The judges will look for a neat, creative, well-organized display. They will want to see a clear and thorough presentation of your data and resources. Finally, they will want to see that you understand your project and can tell them about it clearly and thoroughly. Good luck!

Physical Science 4, SV 3763-1

Name _____ Date _____

Unit 1 Assessment (Part 1)

Decide whether each statement is true or false.
Circle T or F at the right of each statement.

1. Sound travels faster than light.   1.   T   F

2. Sound is a form of energy.   2.   T   F

3. Sound waves hit the eardrum inside   3.   T   F
   the ear to make it vibrate.

4. Pitch is how high or low a sound is.   4.   T   F

5. Sound is measured in units called newtons.   5.   T   F

Read each question. Choose the best answer from those
listed. Write the letter of your choice on the line at the right.

6. Sound is made when an object   6. _____
   a. breaks.   **b.** vibrates.
   c. cools.   **d.** stops.

7. Sound waves   7. _____
   a. move through matter.
   b. spread out in all directions.
   c. start when a vibration is produced.
   d. all of the above.

GO ON TO THE NEXT PAGE ▶

Unit 1 Assessment (Part 2)

8. To make a guitar sound louder, you need to pluck the string
    a. harder.   **b.** faster.
    c. slower.   **d.** softer.

8. _____

9. Sound travels in
    a. zigzags.   **b.** particles.
    c. waves.   **d.** lines.

9. _____

10. Deaf persons can tell if a stereo is on because
    a. they can hear the music.
    b. they can feel the speakers' vibrations.
    c. they can see the sounds.
    d. they see other people sing.

10. _____

11. Music is made of vibrations
    a. that are loud.
    b. that wind blows.
    c. that move at the same rate.
    d. with high pitches.

11. _____

12. Bigger instruments make
    a. squeaky sounds.   **b.** high sounds.
    c. sharp sounds.   **d.** low sounds.

12. _____

13. More vibrations in an instrument means a
    a. higher pitch.   **b.** bigger sound.
    c. softer sound.   **d.** lower pitch.

13. _____

Unit 1 Assessment
Physical Science 4, SV 3763-1

Name _____   Date _____

Unit 2 Assessment (Part 1)

**Decide whether each statement is true or false.
Circle *T* or *F* at the right of each statement.**

1. Light sources are objects that make light.   **1.**   T   F

2. The bouncing of light off an object is
   called reflection.   **2.**   T   F

3. Light travels very slowly.   **3.**   T   F

4. A shadow has the same shape as the
   object making the shadow.   **4.**   T   F

5. Cardboard is an opaque material.   **5.**   T   F

**Read each question. Choose the best answer from those
listed. Write the letter of your choice on the line at the right.**

6. Which of the following makes its own light?   **6.** _____
   a. the Moon   **b.** a firefly
   c. the Earth   **d.** Mars

7. We can see the Moon because   **7.** _____
   a. it reflects light it gets from the stars.
   b. it makes its own light.
   c. it reflects light it gets from the Sun.
   d. the Earth reflects light from the Sun.

GO ON TO THE NEXT PAGE ➤

Unit 2 Assessment (Part 2)

8. Look at the pictures below. Which picture shows how a pencil looks when it is in water?

8. _____

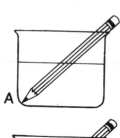
A

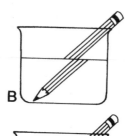
B

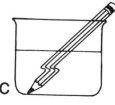
C

D

a. A   **b.** B   **c.** C   **d.** D

---

9. When light passes through a lens, it
   a. moves faster.   **b.** moves slower.
   c. is bent once.   **d.** is bent twice.

9. _____

10. The point where light beams meet after they pass through a lens is called the
   a. mirror.   **b.** prism.
   c. reflection.   **d.** focal point.

10. _____

11. How does a prism separate colors?
   a. It bends each color a different amount.
   b. It bends each color the same amount.
   c. It bends only violet.
   d. It bends only violet and red.

11. _____

12. When all the colors of the spectrum are reflected, an object will look
   a. blue.   **b.** red.
   c. black.   **d.** white.

12. _____

Unit 3 **Assessment** (Part 1)

 **Decide whether each statement is true or false.
Circle *T* or *F* at the right of each statement.**

---

1. This drawing shows a movable pulley.

1.   T   F

2. A flagpole uses a fixed pulley.

2.   T   F

3. A doorknob is the wheel part of a wheel and axle.

3.   T   F

4. All machines use gear wheels.

4.   T   F

5. Smooth surfaces cause more friction than rough surfaces.

5.   T   F

 **Read each question. Choose the best answer from those listed.
Write the letter of your choice on the line at the right.**

---

6. A pulley is a wheel with
   a. a rope that does not move.   **b.** an axle attached to it.
   c. a lever attached to it.   **d.** a rope that moves around it.

6. _____

7. Which of the following is a wheel and axle?
   a. hammer   **b.** screwdriver
   c. scissors   **d.** nail

7. _____

GO ON TO THE NEXT PAGE

Unit 3 Assessment

Unit 3 Assessment (Part 2)

8. Wedges are used to   8. _____
   a. stick things together.   **b.** break things apart.
   c. lift things.   **d.** lower things.

9. A lever can be used to lift a heavy object by   9. _____
   a. pushing down on one end of the bar.
   b. pulling the object with the bar.
   c. rolling the object with the bar.
   d. putting the bar on top of the object.

10. A hammer can be used as   10. _____
   a. a wedge.   **b.** a screw.
   c. a lever.   **d.** an inclined plane.

11. A seesaw is   11. _____
   a. a screw.   **b.** an inclined plane.
   c. a wedge.   **d.** a lever.

12. There is friction whenever   12. _____
   a. two surfaces rub together. **b.** an object does not move.
   c. an object is weighed.   **d.** an object if lifted.

13. A wheel reduces friction because   13. _____
   a. only a small part of it touches the ground at one time.
   b. it moves slowly.
   c. it is square.
   d. it makes things harder to move.

INTRODUCTION

By the fourth grade, students are beginning to explore the world around them. They question the whys and hows of everything they see, taste, touch, feel, and hear. This unit introduces concepts of sound. Students learn how sound is made, how it travels, and how the waves are decoded in our brains. They also begin to understand how instruments produce sound and that different materials and shapes determine a pitch of an instrument. Finally, students learn how scientists use sound waves to map ocean topography.

SOUND

Energy is the use of a force to move an object. Light, heat, and electricity are all forms of energy that cause movement. Sound is another kind of energy that is made from vibrating objects. As an object begins to vibrate, the surrounding molecules also begin to move. Traveling in sound waves, the molecules collide with other objects in their path. The sound energy is transferred to those objects, so they, too, begin to vibrate. When the initial vibration stops, the sound stops.

Vibrations can be heard, seen, and felt. A guitar string, when still, produces no movement or sound, but when plucked, the string moves up and down. You can see the string move, and you can feel it if you lightly place your hand on it. Because the string vibrates, it makes a sound. As the string slows its vibration, the sound dims. As soon as it stops vibrating, the sound stops.

Anything that produces energy can make a sound. The wings of a bee move and create a vibration that produces a buzzing sound. A hammer hits a nail and produces a vibration from the contact. When we speak, air rushes out of the windpipe and collides with the vocal cords, tissues controlled by the muscles of the larynx. This collision causes the vocal cords to vibrate, resulting in sound. These sounds become words when the tongue, teeth, and lips shape the sounds.

Sound Waves

Sound waves are invisible. As the molecules move away in all directions, they travel in a concentric pattern. Their motion resembles the pattern made when a stone is tossed into water; as the circles move out, they get larger. But the energy diminishes as they grow.

A sound wave moves in a longitudinal pattern. It looks much like a spring. The crest is the highest part of the wave, and the trough is the lowest part. The amplitude is the distance halfway between the crest and trough of a sound wave. This characteristic indicates how far molecules move from their origin. An actual wavelength is the distance between two crests. Sound frequency is measured by the number of crests, or vibrations, that move past a point in one second. A high frequency means a greater number of crests past one spot. No sound at all is indicated with a straight line. The human ear can detect frequencies ranging from 20 to 20,000 vibrations per second.

Sound waves also travel through all matter—solids, liquids, and gases, although at varying speeds. The only place sound energy cannot travel is in a vacuum. Most sounds we hear travel through air molecules, a gas. Since gas molecules are loosely packed, sound waves generally travel more slowly through air. The standard rate is 332 meters per second. However, the speed of travel increases with higher temperatures, because the gas molecules are moving faster and colliding at an increased rate. The rate increases 0.6 meters per second for every degree the temperature rises on a Celsius scale.

When sound travels through water, it averages a speed of 1,433 meters per second. Again, the hotter the liquid the faster the sound wave travels. Sound waves travel faster through solids. In steel, they can travel 4,999 meters per second. Native Americans living on the plains often put their ears to the ground to listen for the sound of buffalo. They could get an idea of how large the herd was, in which direction it was traveling, and how quickly the buffalo moved.

Pitch
Pitch is how high or low a sound is. A piccolo is an instrument with a high pitch, while a bassoon has a low pitch. A pitch is the same as frequency. A higher frequency indicates a higher pitch, or sound. A lower frequency has a lower pitch. Moreover, each musical note made by an instrument has its own pitch.

Loudness
Loudness is measured by the amplitude of a sound wave. Shorter amplitudes have a softer sound. Taller amplitudes have a louder sound. The faster and harder an object vibrates, the greater the amplitude of a wave will be, making the sound louder. High-pitched and low-pitched sounds can be soft or loud.

Loudness is measured in units known as decibels. A soft sound, such as breathing, has a decibel reading of 0; it is barely audible. A jet plane's engine has a reading of 160 decibels, a level that is painful to human ears. Any sound that has a reading of more than 130 decibels is dangerous to human ears. Continuous exposure to sounds having high decibels can result in the loss of hearing.

INSTRUMENTS

Instruments produce sound waves in steady, regular intervals. A note is made of a sound that has the same pitch each time. The pitch is controlled by the material the instrument is made of, as well as the size of it. A piccolo, having a high pitch, is a short, small-barreled instrument made of metal. A bassoon is a very long, hook-like instrument made of wood. There are three kinds of musical instruments: wind, string, and percussion. The instruments are grouped by the way the sounds are produced.

Wind

Wind instruments obtain their name because a player blows air from the mouth into the instrument. Wind instruments have two categories. The wood instruments are made of wood. They get their name due to a thin wood piece, called a reed, which produces the vibrations. A musician blows air across the reed. Its vibrations travel the length of the instrument, which is filled with air, transferring its energy to the air molecules inside. The length of the air column is controlled by valves, which open to release air. When more holes are open, the air column is shorter. Thus, the pitch, or musical note, is higher. Flutes, saxophones, clarinets, and recorders are examples of wood instruments.

Brass instruments are also included in the wind-instrument category. A player's lips vibrate to control the air flow into the instrument. It is the vibration of the lips that causes the energy to transfer to the air column in the instrument. Tubas, trombones, and French horns are examples of brass instruments.

String

String instruments have strings. When plucked, hit, or moved with a bow, the strings vibrate. The vibrations are transferred to the surrounding air, thus producing sounds we can hear. Pitch, or the musical notes, are made by changing the length of the strings. The piano, violin, and guitar are examples of string instruments.

Percussion

In a percussion instrument, sound is made when a part of the instrument is hit, either by hand or with another object. That part of the instrument vibrates. The energy is transferred to the surrounding air so that the sound can be heard. The instrument is solid or constructed by stretching material over a hollow container. Cymbals and drums are examples of percussion instruments.

HEARING

The ears help decode the vibrations so that we can hear. The ear is divided into three parts—the outer ear, middle ear, and inner ear. The outside of the ear acts like an inverted megaphone to catch sound waves moving in the air. As the sound waves hit the ear shell, they are reflected inward. The waves move into the auditory canal. The energy of the vibrations is transferred to the air inside the auditory canal. The vibrations hit the tightly stretched tissue of the eardrum, the beginning of the middle ear. It begins to vibrate, passing the energy to three small bones in the ear. The bones increase the vibrations. From there, the vibrations pass to the inner ear. In the inner ear, the vibrations transfer the energy to the liquid-filled cochlea. As the liquid picks up the vibrations, it moves tiny hairs. The hairs change the vibrations into electric signals. The electric signals travel through the auditory nerve to the brain. The brain then decodes the signals to recognizable sounds we can understand.

TECHNOLOGY

Telephones, videotapes, and CD's are all useful technologies that produce sound. Sound energy is transferred to other kinds of energy, such as light, electromagnetic, and electrical energy. Scientists continue to research and utilize these energies to explore the world around us. Oceanographers map the ocean floor using sound waves. Devices called echo sounders send sound waves to the ocean floor. They bounce back to be received on a reciprocating machine. Scientists know the speed that sound travels in water, so they calculate the time it takes for the sound wave to return to the ship. Waves that return quickly indicate the ocean floor is at a shorter distance, perhaps an ocean mountain. Those that take longer to return indicate a deeper ocean depth.

Other advancing technologies help deaf people communicate over the phone. The Telecommunication Device for the Deaf (TDD) system uses a keyboard and a special telephone on which typed words scroll across a window. Deaf individuals communicate directly with each other using their phones and keyboards. To communicate with hearing people, relay stations, manned by operators who hear, link the two. The relay station workers have the TDD telephones and speak the words to the hearing person. The operator types the verbal response, sending it back to the deaf person's TDD phone.

Name _____ Date _____

Hearing Sounds

You use your ears to hear. You can hear the singing of the birds, the soft sound of falling rain, or the loud buzz of an alarm clock. Take a walk in your neighborhood or around the school to listen for sounds you can hear.

✔ **You will need:**

tape recorder   tape   paper   pencil

1. Get a tape recorder, sheet of paper, and a pencil.

2. On the paper, draw a map of the area you are going to visit in your sound search. Draw streets, buildings, and parks on your map.

3. Walk around the area you have chosen to visit. As you walk, record the sounds being made there. Identify the area on the tape.

4. After your walk, listen to the tape. On your map, write the types of sounds you recorded at different locations.

5. Think about the sounds you recorded.

Answer the questions.

1. Were the sounds made by people or animals? _____

_____

2. Were the sounds pleasant or unpleasant? _____

_____

3. Were the sounds natural or unnatural? _____

_____

Sound

Have you ever put your hand on a stereo speaker and felt it shake? Stereo speakers and other things that make sounds vibrate. If you pluck a guitar string or tap a tuning fork, you can see it vibrate back and forth. In fact, sound travels through the air and other matter as a back-and-forth vibration.

You can't see the air around a guitar string or tuning fork vibrate, but if you put a tuning fork in a pan of water, you can see the waves it makes.

Circle the best answer.

1. Suppose a few grains of rice were sitting on top of a bowl that was covered with plastic wrap. If you held a pan near the rice and hit the pan with a spoon, the rice would . . .

   a. rip the plastic wrap.   **b.** fall into the bowl.

   c. shake.   **d.** soften.

2. When you tap a tuning fork, it . . .

   a. does nothing.   **b.** makes a sound.

   c. shakes.   **d.** shakes and makes a sound.

3. Another word for *shaking back and forth very quickly* is . . .

   a. spinning.   **b.** twisting.   **c.** sounding.   **d.** vibrating.

4. Suppose some empty glasses are sitting on a table next to a stereo. Explain why the glasses might rattle when someone turns on the stereo.

   _____

   _____

   _____

How Do Sounds Vibrate?

Sound travels in waves. As the waves move out and away from the place where the sound starts, they push against other objects in their path. As the sound wave hits an object, it causes the object to vibrate. The louder the sound, the harder the sound wave hits.

✔ **You will need:**

plastic bowl	plastic wrap	clear tape	uncooked rice
metal pot	wooden spoon	meter stick	

1. Stretch the plastic wrap across the top of the plastic bowl. Tape the wrap in place, making sure the wrap is pulled as tightly as it can be.

2. Place the bowl on the table. Place about 20 grains of rice on the plastic so they do not touch.

3. Hold the metal pot near the bowl. Hit the pot with the spoon gently. Then hit the pot hard. Watch the rice carefully each time. What happens?

4. Hold the pot about one meter from the bowl. Gently tap the pot with the spoon. What happens to the rice this time?

5. Remove the rice. Hold the pot near the bowl again. Rest your fingers lightly on the plastic wrap. Have a classmate gently hit the pot. Then have your classmate hit the pot harder. Do you feel a difference in the movement of the plastic wrap?

GO ON TO THE NEXT PAGE ➤

How Do Sounds Vibrate?, p. 2

Answer the questions.

1. What made the rice move? _____

2. What happened when the pot was hit gently? _____

_____

3. What happened when the pot was hit hard? _____

_____

4. How close must the pot be to the bowl to make the wrap move?

_____

_____

5. How can sounds make objects move? _____

_____

Unit 1: Sound Off!
Physical Science 4, SV 3763-1

What Is Vibrating?

Look at each picture. What can vibrate to make a sound? Write the name of the object on the line.

1.

   _____

2.

   _____

3.

   _____

4.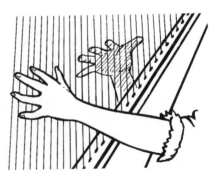

   _____

5.

   _____

6.

   _____

7.

   _____

8.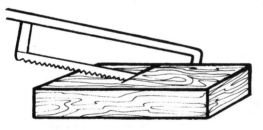

   _____

Feeling Vibrations

When you hum, your vocal cords come close together. As your breath passes out of your throat, it crosses the vocal cords. This moving stream of air causes your vocal cords to vibrate. You can use this moving stream of air to make other things vibrate, too.

 You will need:
comb   piece of wax paper

1. Fold the wax paper in half. Place it over the comb. Tuck the teeth of the comb into the bottom of the fold.

2. Hum softly without the comb.

3. Then put the covered comb between your lips. Hum softly again. Does it sound the same as humming without the comb?

 Answer the questions.

1. What caused the sound to change when you hummed with the comb?

_____

2. Could you hear the vibrations? Explain. _____

_____

3. Could you feel the vibrations? Explain. _____

_____

Name _____   Date _____

Sound and Matter

You know that sound travels through air. Since air is a gas, you know that sound can travel through gases. Have you ever had your head entirely underwater? If you have, you may have noticed that you can still hear things. That's because sound can travel through liquids such as water. Sound can also travel through solids. If you hold a tuning fork upright on a table and put your ear against the table, you can hear the sound the tuning fork makes.

 Answer the questions.

1. Sounds travel through . . .

   a. solids.   **b.** liquids.   **c.** gases.   **d.** solids, liquids, and gases.

2. Why would pressing your ear against the door be helpful if you wanted to hear something on the other side of the door? _____

   _____

   _____

   _____

3. How could someone who is deaf tell whether sounds are coming out of a stereo speaker? _____

   _____

   _____

   _____

Sound in Solids, Liquids, and Gases

Sound can travel through solids, liquids, and gases. However, sound does not travel at the same speed through each kind of matter.

 You will need:

ruler	rubber eraser
tuning fork	water-filled balloon

1. Work with a partner. Stand with your back to your partner. Have the partner strike the tuning fork against the eraser and hold it about 10 cm from your ear. Listen for the sound.

2. Switch places. Repeat Step 1 so that your partner can listen to the sound of the tuning fork.

3. Put your ear against the table. Have your partner strike the tuning fork against the eraser and hold the handle about 20 cm from your head. Listen to the sound. Switch places and repeat.

4. Place the water-filled balloon on the edge of the table. Have your partner strike the tuning fork against the eraser and hold the handle gently to the balloon. (BE CAREFUL NOT TO BREAK THE BALLOON WITH THE TUNING FORK.) Listen for the sound.

 Answer the questions.

1. Did sound travel better through a solid, liquid, or gas? Explain.

   _____

   _____

2. Through which matter did the sound not move as well? Explain.

   _____

   _____

Unit 1: Sound Off!

Physical Science 4, SV 3763-1

Sound and Solids

Sound can travel through a solid object. Does it travel better through some solids than others? Does it travel better through soft materials than hard ones?

 You will need:
pencil   sponge   wooden ruler   metal pot

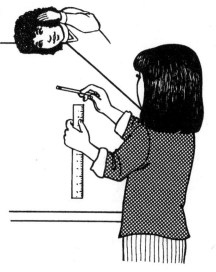

1. Work with a partner. Press your ear to the surface of a table. Cover your other ear with your hand.

2. Your partner should stand at least one meter from you. Have your partner hold a wooden ruler upright on the table, as shown. Your partner should gently tap the top of the ruler with a pencil.

3. Then have your partner hold the sponge on the table. Your partner should tap on the sponge with a pencil. Is the sound louder, softer, or the same as when the ruler was tapped?

4. Next, have your partner tap the metal pot with a pencil. Is the sound louder, softer, or the same as when the ruler was tapped?

 Answer the questions.

1. Which tapped object was the loudest? _____

_____

2. Does sound travel better through some solids than others? Explain.

_____

3. Does sound travel better through soft objects or hard objects?

_____

Name _____   Date _____

Sound Travels at Different Speeds

Sound travels faster through some materials than others.
Read the table below. It shows how fast sound travels through
some common materials in one second.

Speed of Sound

Material	Distance Sound Travels in 1 Second
Water	1,433 meters
Steel	4,999 meters
Granite	6,096 meters
Cork	503 meters
Brick	3,627 meters
Lead	1,219 meters
Iron	4,877 meters
Space	0 meters
Air (at 0°C)	332 meters

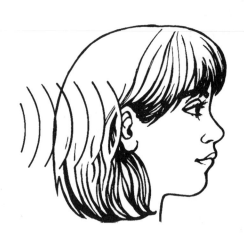

Answer the questions.

1. Does sound travel through space? _____

2. Of the materials listed, through which does sound move the slowest?

_____

3. Does sound move faster through cork or through water?

_____

4. Of the materials listed, through which does sound travel the fastest?

_____

5. How much faster does sound travel through steel than through iron?

_____

6. How much faster does sound travel through granite than through air?

_____

Name _____ Date _____

What Causes Sound to Change?

Sound is made when objects vibrate. The size of the object or the material the object is made of can affect the sound it makes. By changing either the size or the material, sound can change.

☑ **You will need:**
plastic ruler

1. Place the ruler on the edge of a table so that half of it hangs off.

2. Hold the end of the ruler flat against the table with one hand. With the other hand, lightly snap the end of the ruler that hangs off the table. Listen to the sound.

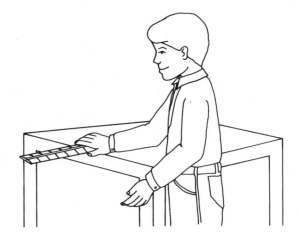

3. Push the ruler back, so that less of the ruler hangs off the table. What do you think will happen to the sound now? Repeat Step 2. Record your observations on the table below.

4. Push the ruler so that most of it hangs off the table. What do you think will happen to the sound now? Repeat Step 2. Record your observations on the table below.

Ruler Sounds

Length	How Sound Changed
Shorter	
Longer	

GO ON TO THE NEXT PAGE ▶

Unit 1: Sound Off!

     Physical Science 4, SV 3763-1

Name _____   Date _____

What Causes Sound to Change?, p. 2

Answer the questions.

1. What happened when you hit the free end of the ruler in Step 2?

   _____

   _____

2. What happened to the sound when the ruler stopped?

   _____

   _____

3. How did the sound change when the ruler was made shorter?

   _____

   _____

4. What happened when the ruler was made longer?

   _____

   _____

5. What causes sound to change? _____

   _____

   _____

Unit 1: Sound Off!

Physical Science 4, SV 3763-1

Name _____ Date _____

How Can You Change the Sound of a Musical Instrument?

A musical instrument makes vibrations at the same rate. String instruments have strings that vibrate. There are two kinds of wind instruments—woodwinds and brass. A woodwind is made of wood. A brass instrument is made of metal. Woodwinds make sounds when air moves across a reed, a thin piece of wood. In brass instruments, sound is made by the vibrations of the player's lips. In both kinds of wind instruments, more sound is made as the air travels along the length of the instrument. Percussion instruments make vibrations when they are hit.

✔ **You will need:**
4 drinking straws   scissors
small glass of water   ruler

1. Make musical instruments out of the straws. Flatten about 3 cm of one end of a straw. Rub the scissors over the edges to make them flat.

2. Cut the corners off each flattened side of the straw. This will serve as the reed of a wind instrument.

3. Dip a finger in the water. Lightly rub your finger over the "reed" of the straw.

4. Blow into the reed. What did you hear?

5. Cut the remaining straws into different lengths. Repeat Steps 1 through 3 to make more wind instruments. Predict how you think the length of each straw will affect how it sounds. Try each one.

How Can You Change the Sound of a Musical Instrument?, p. 2

Answer the questions.

1. What caused the sounds? _____

2. How were the sounds of the longer instruments different from the sounds of the shorter instruments?

   _____

   _____

3. How are your instruments like woodwind instruments?

   _____

   _____

4. What caused the sound when you blew through the straw?

   _____

   _____

5. How did the sounds of the different instruments compare with your predictions?

   _____

   _____

   _____

   _____

Unit 1: Sound Off!

Physical Science 4, SV 3763-1

How Can You Change the Pitch of a Sound?

Pitch is the highness or lowness of a sound. The pitch depends on vibrations. More vibrations mean a higher pitch. A flute has a high pitch, and a bass violin has a low pitch.

✔ **You will need:**

6 glass bottles of the same size
permanent marker   water   wooden stick

1. Line up the bottles in a straight row.

2. Number them 1 through 6 with the permanent marker.

3. Leave the first bottle empty. Pour a small amount of water into bottle 2. Gradually increase the amount of water in the bottles. Fill bottle 6 so that it is almost full.

4. Tap each bottle with the wooden stick. What happens to each bottle? Do you hear different pitches?

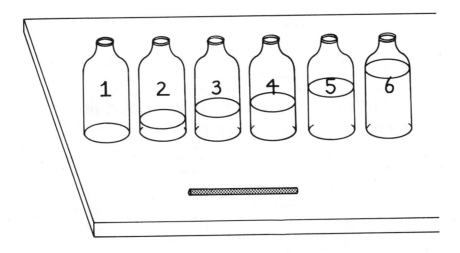

GO ON TO THE NEXT PAGE ▶

How Can You Change the Pitch of a Sound?, p. 2

Answer the questions.

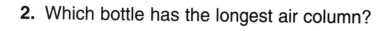

1. Which bottle has the shortest air column?

   _____

   _____

2. Which bottle has the longest air column?

   _____

   _____

3. Which bottle produced the highest pitch?

   _____

   _____

4. Which bottle produced the lowest pitch?

   _____

   _____

5. What is the relationship between the amount of air in a bottle and the pitch of the sound it makes when it is tapped?

   _____

   _____

Unit 1: Sound Off!
Physical Science 4, SV 3763-1

Making a Tambourine

You can make your own musical instruments. When you are finished, you can make your own music. You can also play your instruments to accompany a record.

 You will need:

10 pebbles   stapler   2 large paper plates

1. Place one plate on your desk. Place the pebbles in the center of it.

2. Turn the other plate upside down. Place it on top of the first one.

3. Staple the plates together around the edges. Make sure the staples are close together so that the pebbles do not fall out.

4. To make music, hold the tambourine in one hand. Tap on it with the other.

Answer the questions.

1. How many different sounds do you hear? Name them.

_____

2. What is making each sound?

_____

_____

_____

Making a Kazoo

A kazoo is a musical instrument that is easy to make and fun to play. You can make one easily.

You will need:

a paper roll   wax paper   a rubber band
pencil   centimeter ruler

1. Wrap the wax paper around one end of the tube as shown below.

2. Stretch the rubber band around one end of the tube as shown in the drawing.

3. About 2 cm from the covered end of the tube, make a small hole with the pencil.

4. Hold the open end of the tube to your mouth. Pucker your lips and hum a sound. The kazoo should produce sound.

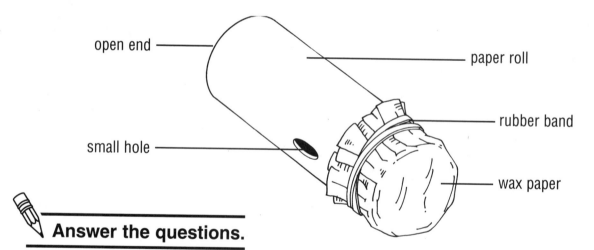

open end ——————
paper roll
rubber band
small hole ——————
wax paper

Answer the questions.

1. What parts of the kazoo vibrate? _____

_____

2. How could you change the sounds from the kazoo? _____

_____

_____

Making a Drum

A drum is a musical instrument. It is part of the percussion family.

You will need:

empty paper oatmeal container
2 pencils   2 rulers   tape

1. Tape the lid tightly onto the oatmeal container.

2. Use the pencils as drumsticks. Use the container as the drum. Try to make loud sounds and soft sounds with your drum.

3. Use the rulers as drumsticks. How are the sounds different?

Answer the questions.

1. What part of the drum vibrates?

   _____

2. How can you change the sound of the drum?

   _____

   _____

Making Rubbing Blocks

Rubbing blocks are one of the oldest kinds of musical instruments.

You will need:
2 blocks of wood (the same size)
sandpaper   glue   scissors

1. Cut two pieces of sandpaper the same size as the top surface of the wood blocks.

2. Glue one piece of sandpaper onto each block. Make sure the rough side of the sandpaper faces up.

3. When the glue is dry, rub the sandpaper sides of the blocks together.

Answer the questions.

1. What part of the rubbing blocks vibrates?

_____

2. What other material could you use in place of the sandpaper? How would the sound change?

_____

_____

How Does Sound Travel?

The energy from a vibrating object goes out in all directions. It bumps the air molecules next to it. These air molecules pass the energy along from molecule to molecule. You can make a model to show how sound waves travel.

✔ **You will need:**

large ball   large piece of paper
16 books of the same size   pencil   ruler

1. Place the paper on the floor. Put the ball in the center of it. While you hold the ball, have a classmate draw a circle around it.

2. Stand the books up in four rows as shown in the picture. The rows must begin just inside the circle you drew on the paper. Put four books in each row. Place each book 5 cm from the book in front of it.

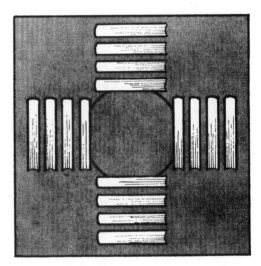

3. Drop the ball into the center of the circle of books.

Answer the questions.

1. What happens when the ball drops in the center of the books?

_____

_____

2. How do sound waves travel?

_____

_____

How Do We Hear?

The pictures show how you hear a dog when it barks. The sentences tell about the pictures. The sentences are not in the correct order. Write numbers to show the correct order of the sentences.

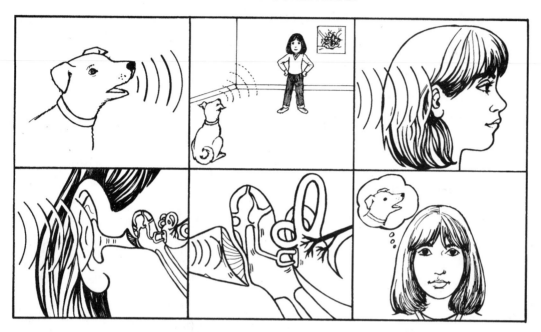

_____ The vibrating vocal cords bump the air molecules. These molecules start to vibrate. Sound waves form. They travel from the dog.

_____ The sound waves push against the eardrum and make it vibrate. The vibrating eardrum passes along the vibrations to three tiny bones, a liquid, and thousands of nerve endings.

_____ The dog barks. Its breath passes out of its throat and makes its vocal cords vibrate.

_____ The outer ear collects the sound waves. It brings them into the narrow canal inside the ear.

_____ Messages about the vibrations are sent along a large nerve to your brain. You recognize the sound as barking.

_____ Sound waves from the dog's vocal cords reach your ears.

Inside the Ear

If you tap a tuning fork softly, it makes a soft sound. If you tap it harder, it makes a louder sound. The same thing happens when you pluck a guitar string. The stronger the vibrations, the louder the sound. The sounds of a tuning fork, guitar, or anything else travel out in all directions. By holding a megaphone to your ear, you can focus more sound toward your ear, making the sounds seem louder. In fact, the outer part of the ear is designed to focus sounds into the ear itself. Many animals have ears that help them hear even better than people do. Once sounds enter the ear, they hit a circle of tissue called the eardrum. When the sound waves hit the eardrum, it vibrates and sends signals through the nerves to the brain. The brain interprets these signals as sounds.

Circle the best answer.

1. If you pluck a guitar string lightly, the sound it makes will be . . .
   a. loud.   **b.** soft.   **c.** high.   **d.** low.

2. To make a guitar sound louder, you need to pluck the string . . .
   a. faster.   **b.** slower.   **c.** harder.   **d.** softer.

3. You can make it easier for someone to hear you if you use a . . .
   a. megaphone.   **b.** tuning fork.   **c.** record player.   **d.** needle.

4. Sounds enter the ear and strike a thin circle of tissue called the . . .
   a. nerves.   **b.** brain.   **c.** cochlea.   **d.** eardrum.

GO ON TO THE NEXT PAGE

Unit 1: Sound Off!

Inside the Ear, p. 2

Look below at the diagram of the ear. The captions under the diagram go with the diagram, but they are out of order. Number them so they are in order. Then decide which part of the diagram each caption describes, and write the number of the correct caption in the circle on the diagram.

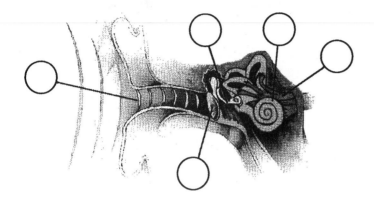

_____ In the cochlea, the vibrations are changed into electric signals.

_____ Sound waves move through the air, hit the outer ear, and are reflected inward.

_____ The electric signals travel through the auditory nerve to the brain, which interprets the signals as sounds.

_____ Within the ear, the sound waves hit a thin circle of tissue called the eardrum, and they make it vibrate.

_____ When the eardrum vibrates, three very small bones move. These bones, in turn, shake the fluid inside a seashell-shaped part of the inner ear called the cochlea.

Making an Eardrum Model

As you may recall, your ear is almost like a megaphone that helps you hear sounds better. As sounds hit your outer ear, they are passed into the inner ear. There they hit the eardrum, which vibrates and sends signals to the brain. Those signals are read by the brain as sounds.

✔ **You will need:**

soup bowl	plastic bag	rubber band
sugar	metal spoon	metal sheet or pan

1. Stretch the plastic bag over the mouth of the bowl until the fit is very tight. Put the rubber band around the bowl to keep the plastic in place.

2. Sprinkle a few grains of sugar onto the plastic.

3. Hold the metal pan close to the bowl. Strike the pan with the spoon. What happens?

_____

_____

_____

_____

GO ON TO THE NEXT PAGE ➤

Making an Eardrum Model, p. 2

1. How is the model you made like an eardrum?

_____

_____

_____

2. When you hear a sound, what is happening?

_____

_____

_____

3. How does the vibrating sugar show that sound waves travel?

_____

_____

_____

4. If you were deaf and looking at the model of the eardrum you just made, how could you tell the loudness of a sound someone made nearby?

_____

_____

_____

_____

Sound Effects

The people who make plays and radio shows often produce their own sound effects. That is, they make a noise with one object, but the sound is like a noise made by something else. For example, to make the sound of an egg frying, they slowly crumple a piece of cellophane. To make the sound of a blazing fire, they crumple the cellophane quickly. You can make your own sound effects.

✔️ **You will need:**

| piece of cellophane | 2 paper cups | pencil | marbles |
| 2 pieces of sandpaper | thick book | paper | glass |

1. To make the noise of an egg frying and a fire blazing, crumple the cellophane.

2. Make the sound of a train locomotive. Rub two pieces of sandpaper back and forth together in a rhythm — CHUG-chug-chug-chug CHUG-chug-chug-chug.

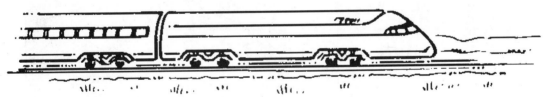

3. To make the sound of a moving horse, hold a paper cup in each hand. Brush the open ends of the cups past each other. Do it in the rhythm of a slow trot. Then try a fast gallop.

To make more sound effects, try the following.
What does each one sound like? Write your ideas.

1. Write on a piece of paper with a dull pencil point. _____

2. Put two marbles in a glass. Spin them around. _____

3. Quickly flip the pages of a thick book. _____

Grouping Sounds

Look at the pictures below. Something in each one is making a sound. Tell whether the object would usually make a loud sound or a soft sound. Under each picture write *loud* or *soft*.

1. _____

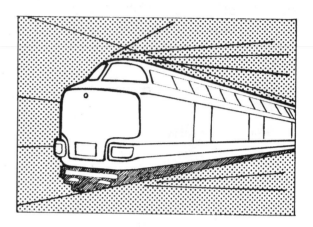

2. _____

3. _____

4. _____

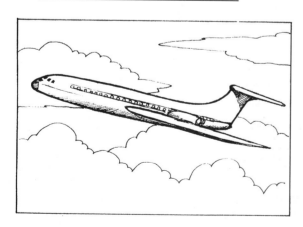

5. _____

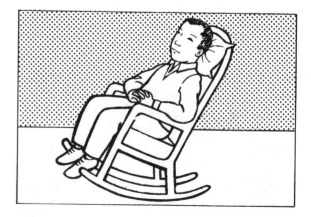

6. _____

Unit 1: Sound Off!
Physical Science 4, SV 3763-1

Decibels

Roaring, humming, honking, giggling—sounds are all around us. Sounds can be pleasing, like a cat purring when you stroke it. And sounds can be annoying, like a phone ringing and ringing. But sounds can also be damaging. Noise can make your head hurt and make you feel bad all over. Very loud sounds can damage your ears and can even make you lose your hearing.

Sound is measured in units called *decibels.* Decibels begin at 0 for sounds that a human with normal hearing would not be able to hear. Something very quiet, such as whispering, is about 10 decibels. As sounds get louder, the number of decibels gets higher. At a certain point, sounds become so loud that they are felt as pain rather than heard as sounds. The chart below shows some common sound levels.

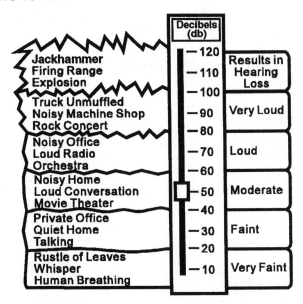

Answer the questions.

1. Sounds that are 100 decibels or higher can cause hearing loss. What sounds might damage hearing?

_____

_____

_____

GO ON TO THE NEXT PAGE ➤

Unit 1: Sound Off!

Physical Science 4, SV 3763-1

Decibels, p. 2

2. What is an example of a sound that is as quiet as whispering?

_____

3. How much louder than whispering is talking?

_____

_____

_____

4. How many decibels do you think a shout would be?

_____

5. What is an example of a sound that is heard at a moderate noise level? How many decibels does this sound measure?

_____

_____

6. Use the space below to make a bar graph of common sounds. Use the data given in the table. You may also add data that you find in reference books.

Echo Sounder

Sound waves can be used to map the bottom of the ocean. An echo sounder is a scientific instrument that sends out sound waves from a ship. The sound waves travel through water until they hit the bottom of the ocean. Then they bounce back to the ship. The time that it takes the sound waves to travel to the ocean bottom and return is measured. Since scientists know how fast sound waves travel in water, they can calculate how far it is to the bottom of the ocean. When sound waves return quickly, it shows that the land is high and there may be a mountain. Sound waves that take a long time to return show that the ocean is deep. There may be a trough.

The line graph below shows an echo sounder reading of an ocean bottom.

Echo Sounder Reading

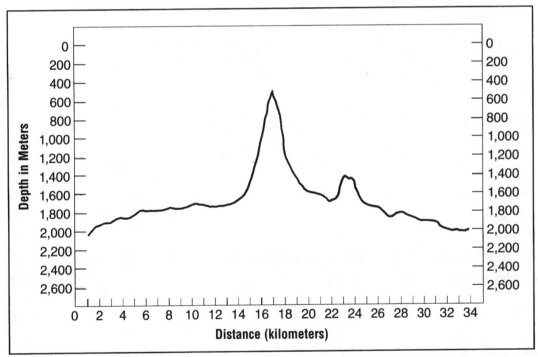

GO ON TO THE NEXT PAGE

Echo Sounder, p. 2

Use the chart on page 49 to answer the questions.

1. How do scientists map the bottom of the ocean?

_____

_____

_____

2. What distance did the scientists map on this chart?

_____

_____

_____

3. At what depth is the top of the underwater mountain?

_____

4. How deep is the deepest part of the ocean shown in the chart?

_____

5. From the deepest part of the ocean, how high is the underwater mountain? _____

6. What are some other reasons that scientists would use an echo sounder to explore the ocean bottom?

_____

The TDD Difference

The phone rings. Not many years ago, a deaf person couldn't use the phone. Today, however, deaf people have a device called a TDD (Telecommunication Device for the Deaf) to help them use the telephone. A TDD phone doesn't work with voices—it works with words. A deaf person who wants to call someone phones that person's TDD number. Instead of talking, the caller types on a keyboard what he or she wants to say. The message appears on the other end of the phone line, on another TDD phone. On most TDD phones, the message appears on a screen on top of the phone. It scrolls across like a message on a screen at a sports event. Sometimes it is printed on paper, instead. The person on the other end reads the message and types in an answer that appears on the TDD phone of the person who called. It's a telephone call typed out on a screen or on paper.

There are several ways for the deaf person on the other end to know that a phone call is coming in. A light might flash to indicate that a call is on the line. Many deaf people who work in offices have fans that turn on and blow air into their faces when the phone rings. Some deaf people have vibrating signals hooked to their beds. When the phone rings at night, the bed vibrates. Other deaf people with TDDs have small devices they can wear that vibrate when they have a call. Still others have specially trained dogs that alert their owners when their owners have calls. There are even answering machines for people with TDD phones. The message is printed out onto paper for the person to read when he or she returns.

Even if you don't have a TDD phone, you can talk to someone who does. Every state now has a relay station so hearing people can communicate with deaf people. The hearing person calls the relay station. A person at the relay station calls the TDD phone of the deaf person and types the message into that machine as the hearing person speaks it.

GO ON TO THE NEXT PAGE ➤

Unit 1: Sound Off!

The TDD Difference, p. 2

1. How do you think TDDs have changed the lives of deaf people?

_____

_____

_____

2. How might a TDD phone make life safer for a deaf person?

_____

_____

3. Do you think it is important to have relay stations that allow a hearing person to talk to a deaf person? Explain.

_____

_____

_____

4. In what other ways do you think deaf people communicate and receive information?

_____

_____

_____

_____

Unit 1 Science Fair Ideas

A science fair project can help you to understand the world around you. Choose a topic that interests you. Then use the scientific method to develop your project. Here's an example:

1. **Problem:** What is the best shape for a megaphone?

2. **Hypothesis:** A cone shape makes sound waves louder.

3. **Experimentation:** Materials: paper, scissors, tape.
   - Make an open-ended cylinder, box, and cone shape out of paper.
   - Have a partner talk in the same voice from the same distance out of each shape.
   - Listen to hear which sound is louder.
   - Repeat, standing at different distances.

4. **Observations:** The cone shape, with the wide part facing out, made the sound louder.

5. **Conclusion:** The best shape for a megaphone is the cone shape.

6. **Comparison:** The conclusion and the hypothesis agree.

7. **Presentation:** Research to find how sound waves travel. Then prepare a presentation or a report to explain your results. Display your shapes and report.

8. **Resources:** Tell the books you used to find how sound waves travel. Tell who helped you to get the materials and set up the experiment.

Other Project Ideas

1. Since bats do not have good hearing, how do they catch food? Do research to find how bats use sound to find insects.

2. For years, children have made toy phones using two tin cans and a long piece of string. Is there a better material to use to conduct sound than string? Experiment using different materials and research information to prove your results.

Unit 2 | LET IT SHINE!

INTRODUCTION

Light is another form of energy. It has many of the same characteristics of sound. Students will learn that light travels in a straight line, but can be reflected by shiny, smooth surfaces. They also discover that light can be bent using flat and curved objects, including mirrors. Finally, students experiment with white light, finding the colors in a spectrum and how rainbows are made.

LIGHT

Light is another form of energy given off in tiny particles called *photons*. Photons are not a kind of matter, but they move in waves. Thus, light energy exhibits characteristics of both particles and waves. Light waves can move through all matter like sound. However, whereas sound cannot move through a vacuum, photons can. Photons move quickly, too, more quickly than anything else in nature. They travel at a rate of about 300,000 kilometers per second through air, whereas sound only travels 334 meters per second. In lightning storms, the lightning is usually seen before the thunder is heard. Though thunder and lightning occur at the same time, we can see lightning before hearing the thunder because light travels so much more quickly than sound.

Light can be produced from both natural and artificial sources. Natural light is produced by the Sun, the most important source, stars, and fireflies. Artificial light is the product of electricity and reactions that can be controlled, such as flashlights, light bulbs, fires, and candles. Some objects appear to be a light source, but they simply reflect a natural light source. The Moon is an example of a reflective object. Light from the Sun strikes the Moon. The light bounces back or reflects, making the Moon look as if it is emitting a light. Because light travels so quickly, the whole process takes about three seconds.

Light from a natural source is called white light. This kind of light cannot be seen. At times it appears that light is visible, but dust particles in the air diffuse the beam, resulting in the visibility of a light beam.

MOVEMENT

Light travels in a straight path from its source, moving away in all directions. But the farther a light beam is from its source, the more the beams diffuse. Light near its source is brighter and more intense, because the photons are more dense. Conversely, the farther you move away from the light source, the dimmer the light appears. Because light has properties of both waves and particles, this decrease in intensity could be due to the photons spreading out or to the waves becoming larger and less concentrated as they move away from the source.

Because light has the tendency to move in a straight line, we cannot see around corners. Moreover, when light hits an object, the object blocks the light, causing a shadow to form. A shadow is the dark area behind an object resulting from the blocking of light waves. Shadows are made when the object is in the path of a light beam. Moreover, the closer the object is to the source, the sharper the shadow will be. The farther an object is from the light source, the more the shadow will be blurred around the edges.

The makeup of the object affects the movement of the light beam. Materials are identified as either transparent, translucent, or opaque. A transparent object, like glass and clear plastic, allows the light to move through, much like a sound wave moves through a solid. Light essentially travels in a straight path through a transparent object. Transparent objects are clear and easily seen through. A translucent object is blurry when you look through it. As light travels through a translucent object, it bends slightly. Because the light bends, the material looks blurry. Opaque objects totally block the light. Since light cannot travel through an opaque object, you cannot see through it.

Reflection and Absorption

Most objects do not produce light. We can see them because of the process of reflection and absorption. Reflection occurs when a light beam collides with an object. The beam bounces back, much like a ball thrown against the floor. When the reflected light hits the eye, we can see the object. Absorption is the process in which a light beam, or parts of a light beam, soak into the object. Some objects absorb part of the beam, while the rest of the beam is reflected. (See the section on Seeing Color.)

Flat Reflectors

The surface of an object also affects the reaction of light. Some surfaces are shiny and smooth. Light reflects, or bounces off, easily. Mirrors and polished metals are good reflectors. When a light beam collides with a reflective surface, the beam bounces back at a corresponding angle. The incoming beam is the angle of incidence, and it is equal to the angle of reflection, the outgoing beam. If the surface is uneven, the beam reacts differently. The particles scatter in all directions. So even if a surface is shiny, it is not a good reflector if the surface is uneven.

Flat mirrors are the best reflectors. The image seen in a mirror is reversed. Moreover, the distance the object is from the mirror is the distance the image appears behind the mirror. Because of their surface, mirrors can easily change the direction of light. Because light bounces off at the same angle it enters, mirrors have multiple functions. Used in pairs, mirrors help us to see beyond barriers and around corners by bending light. Submarine and toy periscopes work because mirrors are parallel to each other and set at 45° angles. Periscopes work because the incoming light bounces to a second mirror. The light is then reflected to the eyes.

Curved Reflectors

Some mirrors are curved. Light reflects off a curved mirror much as it would if a series of flat mirrors were set at angles to each other. As the light particles hit each mirror, they bounce in many directions, but still at an equal angle to the incoming beam. With mirrors curved inward, the light rays can be reflected to a single spot, called a *focal point*. Curved mirrors focus light, making the light brighter and more intense. Flashlights, headlights, microscopes, and telescopes use curved mirrors.

Mirrors can curve in or out. Mirrors curved in, like the inside of a spoon, are called *concave*. The reflection from a concave mirror is larger, because the light rays spread out. On the other hand, the outside of a spoon is an example of a *convex* mirror. It curves out, making an image look smaller. The convex mirror bends light so the rays come together.

Refraction

Light can travel through different materials. The reaction of the light depends on two factors: whether the material is transparent or translucent and what kind of matter the object is. The density of the material affects the speed. A material that is dense will slow the speed of light. When the speed of light changes, it bends. This bending is called *refraction*. Refraction helps us to see transparent objects. For example, light travels through the air and hits glass. Because the glass is clear, light can move through it. However, since it is a different material, the light slows and bends, allowing us to see the glass when the light bends.

Refraction is also the reason for apparent tricks to the eyes, such as a straw in water which looks like it has been cut. Above water, light hits the straw first. But below water, light hits the water and bends before encountering the straw. The bending makes the straw look as if it is cut in half. Likewise, mirages are the result of bending light. On hot days, the air is warmer near a road surface. When light travels from the cool air to warmer air, the light bends because the density of air is different. The result is that we see a puddle of water on the road.

Lenses

Lenses are curved pieces of glass or clear plastic. Like mirrors, lenses can be convex, concave, or flat. Since they have a front and back, they may have a combination of sides, such as a flat front and a concave back. As light moves from the air to the lens, it bends. As the light beam exits the lens, it bends a second time when it enters the air again. Convex lenses are thicker in the middle, and like convex mirrors, bend light to a focal point. The thickness of the glass affects how much the light beam bends. Also, a lens with a sharper curve bends light more sharply. The concave lens is thinner in the middle. It spreads light out.

Many devices utilize lenses. Eyeglasses use both concave or convex lenses to improve eyesight. Microscopes use lenses to make small things look bigger, and telescopes use them so that distant objects seem closer. Cameras also use lenses. The camera lens focuses the light so an image appears on film.

COLOR

Sir Isaac Newton was the first person to discover that light was actually comprised of a spectrum of seven colors: red, orange, yellow, green, blue, indigo, and violet. The spectrum stays in the same color order and can be easily remembered using the name ROY G BIV. Each color has a different wavelength. Red is the longest wavelength, and violet is the shortest. Since the photons travel at different speeds, they bend at different rates as they pass through a transparent object.

Rainbows

A prism is a triangular piece of glass and commonly used to separate colors. Like a lens, light leaves the air and enters the prism, where it slows and bends. As it exits the glass and travels into the air, it bends again. Because the colors move in different wavelengths, they travel at different speeds. They bend at different degrees, resulting in a separation we can see.

Rainbows are created in a similar way, but the raindrops act like prisms. Sunlight enters the drop, and because of the drop's rounded shape, the sunlight reflects back to the front. As it leaves the drop, it bends again. The process causes the sunlight to spread out even more. With millions of drops refracting and reflecting sunlight, a rainbow appears.

Seeing Colors

As white light collides with an object, the whole color spectrum also hits the object. The object reflects its color, absorbing all other colors of the white light. In other words, a yellow ball appears yellow because the yellow wavelength reflects back to our eyes. The other colors are absorbed. To appear white, a white object reflects the entire spectrum. To appear black, the black object absorbs all the colors. When an object is transparent, such as a green glass vase, the green light passes through instead of being reflected; the other colors are absorbed by the glass.

How We See

The eyeball is covered by a cornea, which is a protective film covering the eye. The colored circle on the eye is the iris. The pupil, the black circle, is inside the iris. The iris enlarges and shrinks the pupil to control the amount of light that enters the inside of the eyeball. The pupil shrinks in bright light to reduce the amount of light and enlarges when more light is needed to see. Once light enters the pupil, it moves through the lens. The cornea and the lens work together to bend the light so the reflection focuses on the retina in the back of the eye. The image appears on the retina. From there, the message moves through the optic nerve to the brain. The brain then interprets the message as a picture.

When a part of the eye is not working or the eyeball changes shape, people may have trouble seeing; the image is not being focused on the retina. In nearsighted people, people who have difficulty seeing distant objects, the focus is in front of the retina. Glasses with concave lenses can fix the problem, altering the focus point farther back on the retina. In farsighted people, the light focuses behind the retina. Glasses with convex lenses can help bring the focal point to the retina.

Technology

There are other forms of light, too. X-rays, microwaves, and radio waves are examples of other kinds of light. Our eyes are unable to see or know when this form of energy is near. These forms of light can pass through all forms of matter, gas, liquid, and solid.

Lasers are another form of light energy. A laser is a narrow, but intense, beam of light. Because of the speed and precision of this energy, lasers are used to cut diamonds and communicate with space satellites. The medical community uses lasers as surgical tools, often aiding in the cutting and repairing of delicate organs.

Light Sources

Light is a form of energy made by the Sun, the stars, light bulbs, fires, and fireflies. We can see other objects because the light from a light bounces off, or reflects, and hits our eyes. The Moon is an example of reflection. Light from the Sun hits the Moon and bounces back so we can see it.

Look at the objects below. Write _light source_ or _reflects light_ to tell which objects give off light.

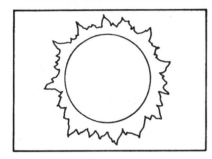  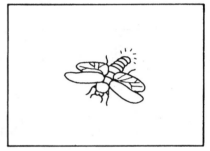

1. _____ 2. _____ 3. _____

4. _____ 5. _____ 6. _____

Name _____   Date _____

Can You See a Light Beam?

You need light to see. If there is no light, you cannot see. And while you can get along without being able to see, it is not easy. In order for you to see something, there must be light shining on it. The light reflects, or bounces off, the object and travels to your eyes. This reaction is similar to the way a ball bounces off a wall.

 You will need:

flashlight   spray bottle filled with water

1. Find a room in which no light can enter. Turn off the lights. What do you see?

2. Turn the flashlight on. Shine it across the room. What do you see?

3. Spray some water where you think the light beam is.

 Answer the questions.

1. When you turned on the flashlight, did you see a light beam?

_____

2. When did you see a light beam? _____

3. How does the water help you to see the light beam? _____

_____

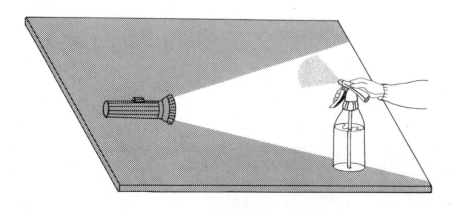

Does Light Travel in a Straight Line?

Like sound, light moves out in all directions from its source. It moves very fast. If something blocks the light, the light is reflected back. The blocked object makes a shadow behind. A shadow is a dark place that has the shape of the object. Because of the shadows, we know that light travels in a straight line.

 You will need:

3 index cards   clay   flashlight   ruler

1. With the index cards held together, punch a hole through them. Make sure the hole is in the same spot on each.

2. Place clay balls in a straight line about 5 cm apart from each other.

3. Stick a card in each ball. Try to line up the holes.

4. Shine the light through the holes. Hold your hand open behind the last card.

5. Slide the second card to one side. What do you see?

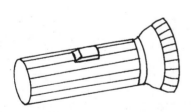
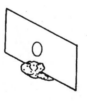

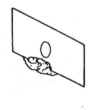

GO ON TO THE NEXT PAGE ➡

Name _____   Date _____

Does Light Travel in a Straight Line?, p. 2

Answer the questions.

1. Did the light travel through the holes when they were lined up?

_____

2. What happened to the light when you moved the middle card?

_____

_____

_____

3. When did you see shadows? Explain.

_____

_____

_____

4. Does light travel in a straight line? How do you know?

_____

_____

_____

5. What happens to light when it is blocked by an object?

_____

_____

_____

_____

Unit 2: Let It Shine!
Physical Science 4, SV 3763-1

Does Light Spread Out from Its Source?

When light is near its source, it is very bright. As it moves out in all directions, it gets dimmer the farther it is from its source. It also spreads out more.

> ☑ **You will need:**
> flashlight   centimeter graph paper   ruler   pencil

1. Work with a partner. Lay the graph paper flat on a table. Hold the flashlight straight up and down. Hold the ruler beside it. Make sure the flashlight is 2 cm from the paper.

2. Look at the circle of light. Have your partner mark four sides, opposite to each other, on the paper.

3. Raise the flashlight to 4 cm. Repeat Step 2.

4. Continue to raise the flashlight 2 cm at a time and mark the light circles until the light reaches the edge of the paper.

5. Turn off the flashlight. Use the ruler to measure the diameter, the distance from side to side, of each circle.

6. Record the diameter measurements in the table on the next page.

GO ON TO THE NEXT PAGE ➡

Does Light Spread Out from Its Source?, p. 2

Measurement of Light

Distance to Paper	Diameter of Light Circle
2 cm	
4 cm	
6 cm	
8 cm	
10 cm	

Answer the questions.

1. What happened to the circle of light as you moved the flashlight away from the paper?

   _____

   _____

2. What happened to the brightness of the light?

   _____

   _____

3. What two things happen to light as it gets farther from its source?

   _____

   _____

Sun Time

Watching how shadows move can help you to tell time. Look at the drawing below. A straw was placed on a piece of cardboard. The cardboard and straw were in the Sun for the whole day. Each hour on the hour, a student drew a line from the bottom of the straw to the tip of the shadow. The student then recorded the hour of the day.

Answer the questions.

1. Predict where the shadow will be 30 minutes after the last measurement. Draw a line on the diagram to show your answer.

2. Predict where the shadow will be one hour after the last measurement. Draw a line to show your answer.

3. Why does the straw cast a shadow?

   _____

4. How can this device be used to tell time?

   _____

   _____

   _____

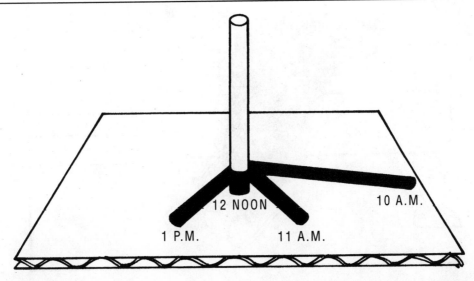

Unit 2: Let It Shine!

Name _____   Date _____

Transparent, Translucent, Opaque

Light doesn't pass through all materials with the same ease. Clear glass and water allow almost all light to pass through them; they are called transparent materials. Thin fabric and frosted glass allow only some light to pass through them; they are called translucent materials. Brick, metal, and thick paper let no light pass through them; they are called opaque materials.

Look at the picture below. Decide whether each arrow points to an object that is transparent, translucent, or opaque. Write the correct word on each line.

Unit 2: Let It Shine!

When Light Strikes

You can tell whether an object is transparent, translucent, or opaque by the type of shadow it casts. A transparent object casts no shadow. Light passes right through it. An opaque object casts a sharp shadow. All the light is blocked by the object. A translucent object casts a blurred shadow. Some of the light is blocked or scattered as it passes through.

 You will need:

set of 4 clear plastic glasses	water	waxed paper
brown wrapping paper	flashlight	blue food coloring
permanent marker		

1. Label the glasses 1, 2, 3, and 4. Leave glass 1 empty. Add water and blue coloring to glass 2. Wrap the brown paper around glass 3. Wrap the waxed paper around glass 4.

2. Shine the flashlight beam at each glass. Observe what kind of shadow forms. Record your observations in the chart below.

Shadows of Objects

Glass	Shadow Formed	Object Is
1		
2		
3		
4		

 Answer the questions.

1. Which object(s) is transparent? _____

2. Which object(s) is translucent? _____

3. Which object(s) is opaque? _____

Reflecting Light

You cannot see someone who is hiding around a corner, even though you may be able to hear the person. Light travels in a straight line; but with a mirror, you can see someone hiding around the corner. When light hits a mirror, it bounces off and changes direction.

You will need:

2 mirrors   a coin   tape

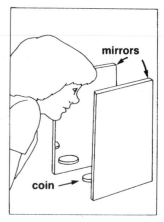

NOTE: This experiment must be done with an adult.

1. Stand the two mirrors on edge facing each other. Place the coin between the mirrors. Look in one mirror. Then look in the other mirror. What do you see?

2. Hinge the two mirrors together with a piece of tape. Set them on edge at an angle to each other. Place a coin between the two mirrors. Observe the number of images formed as you increase and decrease the angle between the mirrors.

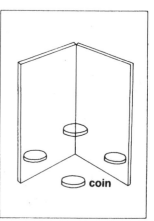

Answer the questions.

1. How many images did you see in the mirror in Step 1?

_____

_____

2. How many images did you see in Step 2?

_____

3. What happened as you increased the angle?

_____

_____

Bouncing Light

When a beam of light hits an object that reflects, the beam bounces off, or reflects, at the same angle it hits, if the surface is smooth. However, if the surface is uneven, the light bounces off in many different angles. The drawings below show how light reflects on a smooth surface and an uneven surface.

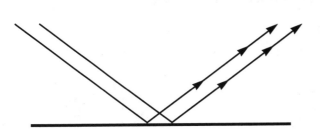
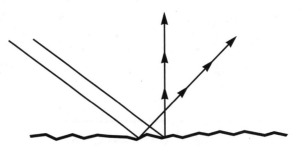

Complete each drawing below to show the path of light after it is reflected.

1.

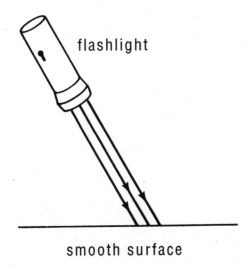

smooth surface

2.

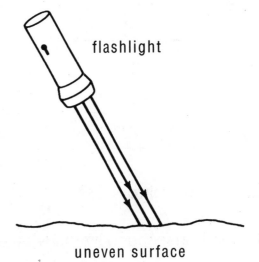

uneven surface

Unit 2: Let It Shine!

Periscope

There are tools that use the properties of light. One of these tools is the periscope. A periscope uses two mirrors to bend the path of light. When the light enters one end of the periscope, it hits a mirror and is reflected toward the mirror on the other end of the periscope. That mirror then reflects the beam out a hole. You can use a periscope to peek over a wall or around a corner. Submarines use periscopes to see above the surface of the water.

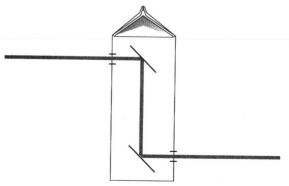

 Answer the questions.

1. Describe the path a beam of light takes when you use a periscope to see someone around a corner.

   _____

   _____

   _____

   _____

   _____

   _____

   _____

2. What do mirrors do? _____

   _____

3. In a periscope, how many times is the light reflected? _____

4. What would happen if the angle of one mirror was changed? _____

   _____

   _____

What Will Make a Good Reflector?

Good reflectors usually have shiny, smooth surfaces. They must be shiny so that the light will bounce back. They must be smooth so that the light will stay together and not scatter. You will not be able to see the beam as clearly when it scatters.

✔ **You will need:**
   flashlight   mirror   2 squares of foil

1. Crumple one sheet of foil so the surface is uneven. Then flatten it out.

2. Hold the mirror in one hand and the flashlight in the other. Stand next to a wall. Aim the light on the mirror so that a reflection shines on the wall. What do you see?

3. Repeat Step 2 using the smooth foil. How does it compare to the reflection you saw using the mirror?

4. Repeat Step 2 using the crumpled foil. How does it compare to the reflections you saw using the mirror and smooth foil?

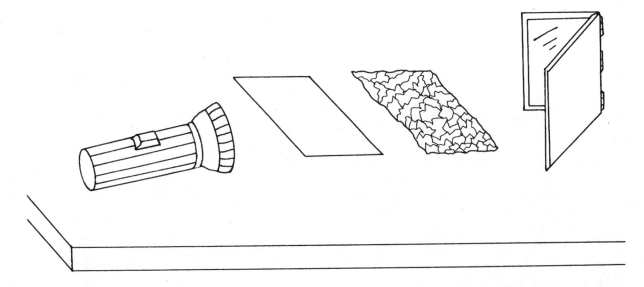

GO ON TO THE NEXT PAGE ➤

Unit 2: Let It Shine!

What Will Make a Good Reflector?, p. 2

Answer the questions.

1. Which material reflected the beam of light best? Explain.

_____

_____

_____

2. Which material reflected the beam of light the least? Explain.

_____

_____

_____

3. Which material makes the best reflector? Why?

_____

_____

4. Which piece of foil reflected better? Why?

_____

_____

5. What other materials would make good reflectors?

_____

_____

_____

Unit 2: Let It Shine!

How Can a Mirror Change the Direction of Light?

If you throw a ball on the ground, the direction it will bounce depends on the angle that the ball hits the ground. Light will bounce like a ball. The angle that it reflects depends on the angle at which the light beam hits the reflector.

✔ You will need:

light box or flashlight   mirror
black paper   white or yellow crayon

1. Put the light box or flashlight on a table. Turn it on. Darken the room.

2. Hold the mirror in the path of the light beam.

3. Move the mirror so that the beam of light hits it at different angles. What do you see?

4. Now place the sheet of black paper under the mirror.

5. Bounce the light beam off the mirror at an angle.

6. Draw a line along the edge of the mirror. Then draw a line to show the path of the light beam hitting the mirror. Draw another line to show the reflected beam.

7. Change the angle of the mirror. Repeat Step 6.

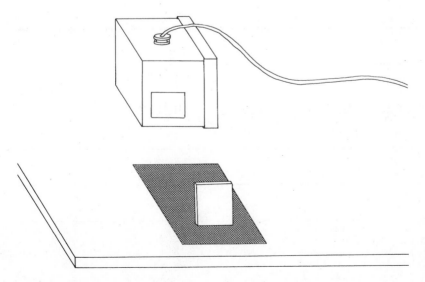

GO ON TO THE NEXT PAGE ▶

How Can a Mirror Change the Direction of Light?, p. 2

Answer the questions.

1. What happened to the light beam when you changed the angle of the mirror?

   _____

   _____

   _____

2. Look at your diagram of the angle of the light beam hitting the mirror. Look at the angle of the reflected beam. How do the angles compare?

   _____

   _____

   _____

3. How does a mirror affect a beam of light?

   _____

   _____

   _____

4. How can you use a mirror to change the direction of a beam of light?

   _____

   _____

   _____

Special Effects

Glass can reflect light and also let it pass through. You can use this fact to make special effects. You can make a candle appear to burn in a glass of water.

✔ **You will need:**

piece of clean glass at least 20 cm x 25 cm
2 thick books, about the same size   tall, clear plastic tumbler
candle in a small candleholder   2 sheets of paper
tape   water   ruler   matches

NOTE: This experiment must be done with an adult.

1. Tape the edges of the glass. Stand the piece of glass between the two thick books, as shown. Place a sheet of paper on top of each book. Make sure the paper is pushed right up against the edge of the glass.

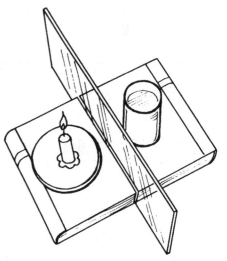

2. Fill the tumbler with water. Place it in the center of one of the books.

3. Put the candle and holder on top of the other book.

4. Using your ruler, measure how far the tumbler is from the glass. Place the candle the same distance from the glass.

5. Have your teacher light the candle. Turn out the lights and pull down the shades.

6. Look at the tumbler of water through the glass. DO NOT GET CLOSE TO THE CANDLE. Move around slowly until you see a reflection. What do you see?

GO ON TO THE NEXT PAGE ▶

Unit 2: Let It Shine!

Special Effects, p. 2

Answer the questions.

1. What do you see when you complete Step 6?

   _____

   _____

2. Why do you think it happens? _____

   _____

   _____

3. How is the glass a reflector? _____

   _____

   _____

4. What other image do you see when you look in the glass? _____

   _____

   _____

5. Why can you see another image? _____

   _____

   _____

Kaleidoscope

In a kaleidoscope, mirrors reflect light from colored objects. Beautiful designs are the result. You can make a kaleidoscope.

✔ **You will need:**

2 long, narrow mirrors (same size)
sheet of heavy cardboard   sheet of thin cardboard
tape   glue   wax paper
plastic wrap   scissors   ruler
2 rubber bands   colored paper   pencil

1. Place one mirror on the thin cardboard. Trace around the outside of the mirror. Make two more outlines next to the first. Leave about $\frac{1}{2}$ cm space between the outlines.

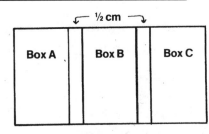

2. Draw a single box around the entire outer edge of all three mirror tracings, as shown. Then cut out the large box.

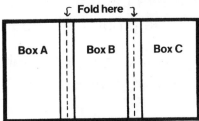

3. Fold the cardboard between Box A and Box B. Fold it again between Box B and Box C. Then unfold it.

4. Glue one mirror onto Box A and one onto Box C. Make sure the mirror sides are up. Let them dry.

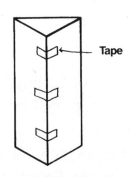

5. Stand the mirrors and cardboard on one end. With the mirror sides facing inward, refold the cardboard to form a triangle. Tape the edges of the cardboard together.

6. Lay the triangle on the heavy cardboard, as shown. Draw a strip lengthwise on the heavy cardboard. Make it as wide as the length of the triangle. Cut out the strip.

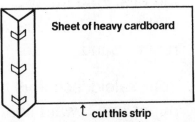

GO ON TO THE NEXT PAGE ➤

Unit 2: Let It Shine!

Kaleidoscope, p. 2

7. Place the triangle on the strip you have just cut out. Wrap the cardboard strip around the triangle to make a tube. Tape the tube shut.

8. At one end of the tube, tape the triangle to the tube. Stand the tube upright on a piece of colored paper. Trace around it with your pencil to make a circle the same size as the end of the tube. About 5 cm outside the first circle, draw another circle around the first. Cut out the larger circle.

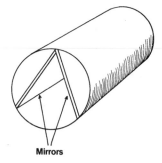

Mirrors

9. Use the large circle as a pattern. Trace a circle on the plastic wrap and on the wax paper. Cut out both circles.

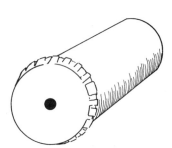

10. Place the colored circle over the end of the tube where the triangle is taped. Fold the sides of the circle around the tube. Tape the paper to the tube.

11. To make a viewing hole, push your pencil through the center of the circle.

12. Place the plastic wrap circle over the other end of the tube. Pull it tight. Tape the wrap to the outside of the tube.

13. Cut out 15 tiny bits of colored paper—about the size of the pencil eraser. Place the tube upright with the plastic wrap end up. Place the paper bits on top of the plastic wrap. Put the wax paper circle on top of the bits. Fold the wax paper tightly around the sides of the tube. Hold the wax paper in place with a rubber band.

14. Your kaleidoscope is now ready to use. Point the wax paper end toward light. Look through the viewing hole. Tap the tube near the wax paper end to see different designs.

Unit 2: Let It Shine!
Physical Science 4, SV 3763-1

How Can Flat Mirrors Focus Light?

Some mirrors are curved. Though they are shiny and the surface is smooth, their shape causes light beams to bend at different angles. Curved mirrors are like many flat mirrors joined together to make a curve. Mirrors that curve inward can focus light. This means that the light beams are bent, or reflected, so that they hit the same spot.

✔ **You will need:**

| light box or flashlight | 3 small mirrors | black paper |
| 5 x 7 index card | clay | ruler |

1. Place the sheet of black paper about 40 cm from the flashlight.

2. Make a screen of the index card by bending the long edge. Place it beside the black paper.

3. Turn on the flashlight and darken the room.

4. Use clay to stand one mirror in the light.

5. Turn the mirror so that the light is reflected on the index card.

6. Place a second mirror next to the first. Turn it so that it reflects light onto the same place on the index card.

7. Using the last mirror, repeat Step 6.

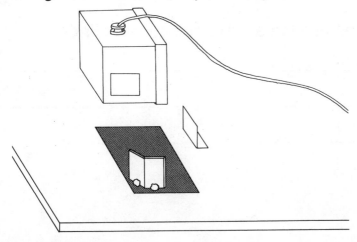

GO ON TO THE NEXT PAGE ▶

Unit 2: Let It Shine!

How Can Flat Mirrors Focus Light?, p. 2

Answer the questions.

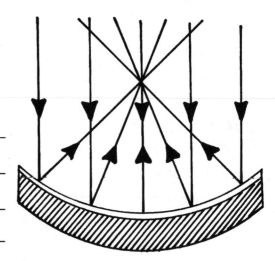

1. What happened to the light hitting the index card when the second mirror was added?

   _____

   _____

   _____

   _____

2. What happened when the third mirror was added?

   _____

   _____

   _____

3. How can flat mirrors be used to focus light?

   _____

   _____

   _____

4. How can several flat mirrors be used to act like one curved mirror?

   _____

   _____

   _____

Curved Mirrors

Curved mirrors are like flat mirrors joined together. When light hits, it reflects at different angles. A flashlight has a concave mirror, and stores have security mirrors that are convex.

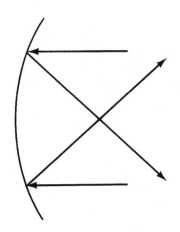 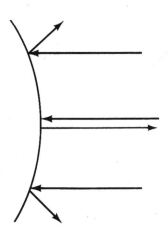

 Answer the questions.

1. What is the difference between a convex mirror and a concave mirror?

_____

_____

_____

2. How is a curved mirror used in a flashlight?

_____

_____

_____

3. How is a convex mirror used in a store?

_____

_____

_____
GO ON TO THE NEXT PAGE ▶

Unit 2: Let It Shine!

         Physical Science 4, SV 3763-1

Curved Mirrors, p. 2

Light bounces off flat and curved surfaces. In each of the diagrams below, show the path of the reflected beam of light.

1.

2.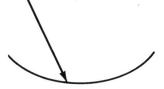

3.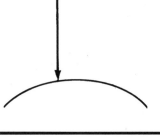

Answer the questions.

4. Name an instrument that uses each of the above mirrors.

_____

_____

5. Which of the above mirrors might be used in a fun house?

_____

6. Which mirror would be used in a car headlight to make a beam of light?

_____

_____

Concave and Convex Mirrors

Mirrors that curve inward are concave mirrors. They reflect light so that it is focused in one spot. Images reflected in the concave mirrors look larger. A spoon is an example of a concave mirror. Convex mirrors curve outward. The reflected light scatters out in a semicircle, making images look smaller. Security mirrors that hang near the ceiling of stores are convex mirrors.

 You will need:
concave mirror
convex mirror

1. Hold the convex mirror in front of your face. Move it closer. Move it farther away.

2. Record what happened in the table below.

3. Hold the concave mirror in front of your face. Move it closer. Move it farther away.

4. Record what happened in the table below.

How I Look in Different Mirrors

Mirror	Close Up	Far Away
Convex		
Concave		

GO ON TO THE NEXT PAGE ➤

Name _____   Date _____

Concave and Convex Mirrors, p. 2

Answer the questions.

1. How are the shapes of the mirrors different?

_____

_____

2. How does an image in a convex mirror look?

_____

_____

3. How does an image in a concave mirror look?

_____

_____

Look at the pictures below. Label each mirror to tell if it is
flat, *concave*, **or** *convex*. **Also write if the image would be the**
same, *smaller*, **or** *larger*.

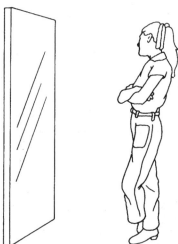  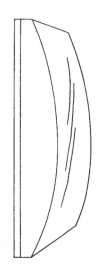  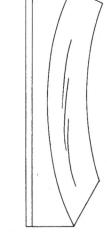 

4. _____   **5.** _____   **6.** _____

Unit 2: Let It Shine!

© Steck-Vaughn Company   Physical Science 4, SV 3763-1

How Can You Bend a Light Beam?

Light can travel through some objects. When light passes from one material to the next, it bends. The kind of material the object is made of slows the speed of light. Because of the change in speed, light is bent. If you have ever seen a straw in a clear cup of water, the straw looks as if it is broken. The speed of light as it passes from air to water changes, making the straw look as if it is cut in half at the water's surface.

✔ **You will need:**

light box or flashlight	water	black paper
clear, plastic shoe box	milk	spray bottle

1. Place the shoe box on the black paper. Fill the shoe box with water.

2. Mix 4 or 5 drops of milk in the water.

3. Shine the light through one long side of the shoe box.

4. Spray some water in the beam of light. Look down from above. What do you see?

5. Try to bend the light by moving the flashlight to a new position. What happens now?

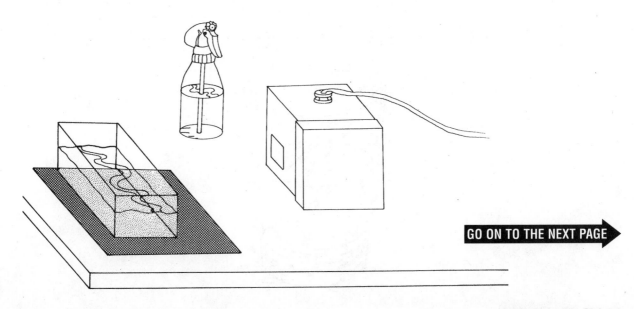

GO ON TO THE NEXT PAGE ➡

Unit 2: Let It Shine!

How Can You Bend a Light Beam?, p. 2

Answer the questions.

1. What happens to the light beam when the flashlight points straight to the side of the shoe box? _____

_____

2. If you change the angle of the flashlight, what happens?

_____

_____

3. What can you change to make the light beam bend even more?

_____

_____

4. Look at the picture below. Explain why the pencil looks broken.

_____

_____

_____

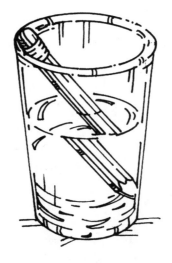

Unit 2: Let It Shine!

Lenses Bend Light

A lens is a piece of curved glass or plastic material that bends light beams. Where the light beams meet is the focal length. The angle that a beam bends depends on the shape and the thickness of the lens. A thicker lens will have a shorter focal length. When the light enters one side of the lens, it bends as it passes from air to glass or plastic. It bends a second time as the light leaves the glass and enters the air.

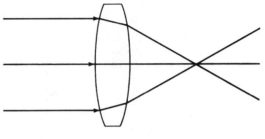

Answer the questions.

1. How is a lens like a curved mirror? _____

_____

_____

2. Why are lenses made of transparent materials? _____

_____

_____

3. How does a lens bend light? _____

_____

_____

4. Name three objects that use lenses. _____

_____

_____

Objects That Use Lenses

A. Look at the picture. Hidden in it are five objects that use at least one lens. Find the eyeglasses, a telescope, a microscope, a magnifying glass, and a camera.

B. Read about the objects in the picture. Decide which object each group of sentences describes. Write its name on the line.

1. _____ A lens and a lens holder are its only parts. The lens is thicker in the middle than at the edges. It collects light and brings it together on one spot. It makes close-up objects appear bigger.

2. _____ Two lenses help focus light on the retina. The lenses may help a nearsighted person see distant objects.

3. _____ It is a special box with a lens in front. Inside the box is a film. The lens gathers light from outside the box. When set properly, it focuses a clear, sharp image on the film.

4. _____ It has a long tube with a lens at each end. The lenses work together. They make tiny things that are placed close to one lens appear much bigger.

5. _____ Its long tube has a lens at each end. The lenses work together. They make faraway objects look bigger and closer.

Unit 2: Let It Shine!

How Glasses Work

Have you ever heard the term *nearsighted*? A person who is nearsighted has trouble seeing things far away but has no problem seeing things that are nearby. A person who is *farsighted* has the opposite problem and has trouble seeing things that are close.

What causes a person to be nearsighted or farsighted? Both problems may be caused by the shape of the eye or by problems in the cornea or the lens. In normal vision, light rays travel from an object to a person's eye. In the eye, the light rays pass through the cornea and the lens. These two parts of the eye bend the light rays together and focus them on the retina at the back of the eye. An image of the object forms on the retina. Look at the drawing to see how this happens.

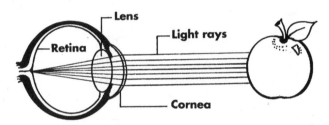

When a person has vision problems, it is often because light is not being focused onto the correct spot inside the eye. If a person is nearsighted, the light rays come together, or focus, before they reach the retina. A person is usually nearsighted because his or her eyeballs are a little too long. This vision problem can be corrected with glasses that change the place where the light rays come together. These glasses have concave lenses. A concave lens is thinner in the middle than it is on the edges.

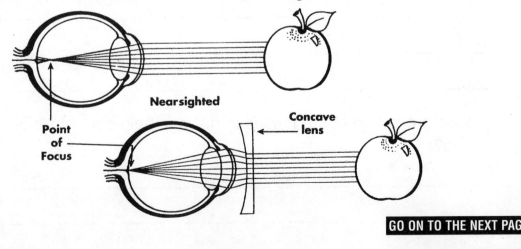

GO ON TO THE NEXT PAGE ➡

Unit 2: Let It Shine!

How Glasses Work, p. 2

When a person is farsighted, the light rays focus on a spot beyond the retina. This may be because the eye is a little too short. When people get older, they often become farsighted because the lenses of their eyes are no longer able to focus as well as when they were younger. Farsightedness can be corrected with glasses that have convex lenses, which are thicker in the middle than on the edges. These glasses also change the point at which light rays come together.

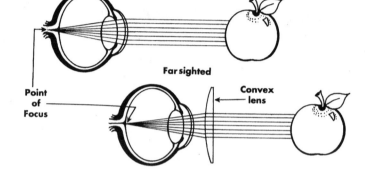

Far sighted

Point of Focus

Convex lens

Answer the questions.

1. Explain how light is focused for normal vision.

   _____

   _____

   _____

   _____

2. Explain how light is focused in the eyes of people who are nearsighted and people who are farsighted. _____

   _____

   _____

   _____

3. How does the shape of the lenses in glasses help correct vision problems? _____

   _____

   _____

Unit 2: Let It Shine!

Magnifying with Water

A magnifying glass makes objects look bigger. You don't need a magnifying lens to make objects appear bigger. Water will work, too. You can make a water magnifier.

✔ You will need:

tall, thin glass bottle with round sides, such as an olive bottle
2 pencils (same size)   water   other glass jars with round sides

---

1. Put one pencil in the tall, thin bottle. Hold the other pencil against the outside of the bottle. Look through the side of the bottle. Compare the pencils. Does one appear bigger than the other?

2. Fill the bottle 3/4 full of water. Hold the pencil outside the bottle again. Look through the side of the bottle. Compare the sizes of the two pencils.

3. Hold the pencil near the front of the bottle. Then hold it near the back of the bottle. When does it look bigger?

4. Test other glass containers with round sides. Find out which one makes the best magnifier.

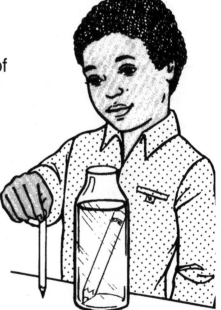

A glass container with round sides holds the water in the shape of a convex lens. Light that travels through the container is bent. The container and the water act like a convex lens. They can make larger images of objects.

White Light and Prisms

Light that comes from a natural source is white light. When it passes into glass or water, the speed slows and the beam bends. White light that enters a prism, a triangular piece of glass, bends in the glass, and then bends again when leaving the glass. The result is a spectrum, seven colors that make up light. The colors are red, orange, yellow, green, blue, indigo, and violet. The color red bends the least in a prism, while violet bends the most.

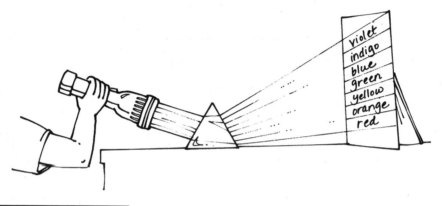

Answer the questions.

1. What happens when white light passes through a prism? _____

_____

_____

_____

2. What is a spectrum? _____

_____

3. How is a raindrop like a prism? _____

_____

4. How is a rainbow made? _____

_____

_____

What Is White Light Made Of?

White light is light that comes from a natural source. It is clear and generally not seen. When this kind of light passes through glass or water, it changes speed and bends, producing a spectrum of seven colors.

✔ **You will need:**

flashlight or sunlight   mirror   tape
white paper   tray of water
crayons (red, yellow, blue, green, orange, violet, purple)

1. Place the tray of water near a wall. Set the mirror in the water.

2. Tape a piece of white paper on the wall.

3. Shine the flashlight at the mirror. Move the flashlight around until you can see a reflection on the paper. What colors do you see?

4. Use your crayons to draw the order of the colors on the next page.

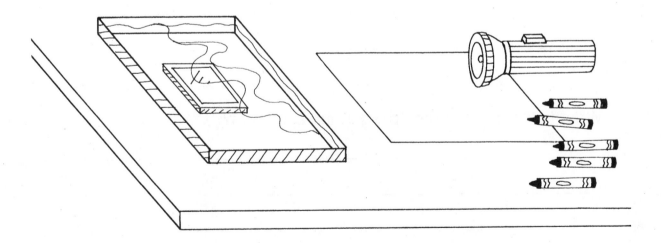

GO ON TO THE NEXT PAGE ➤

What Is White Light Made Of?, p. 2

Spectrum of Colors

Answer the questions.

1. How did the water help to make the spectrum?

_____

_____

_____

2. How did the mirror help to make the spectrum?

_____

_____

_____

3. What is the order of the colors in the spectrum?

_____

_____

_____

4. Do you think the order of the spectrum changes? Explain.

_____

_____

_____

What Happens When Light Hits an Opaque Object?

White light is made up of seven colors. When the light hits an object, all the colors in the white light hit the object, too. If all the colors bounce off, the object looks white. In colored objects, that color of the white light is reflected back to our eyes. Thus, we can see that color. All the other colors soak into, or are absorbed by, the object. For example, we see a blue ball because the blue light in the spectrum reflects to our eyes. The other colors are absorbed, so we cannot see them.

✔ You will need:

white, red, green, blue construction paper
flashlight

1. Lay the white paper on a table. Turn on the flashlight. Darken the room.

2. Hold a sheet of colored paper at an angle to the white paper.

3. Shine the flashlight onto the colored paper. Gradually change the angle of the colored paper, making it smaller. What do you see on the white paper?

4. Record your findings on the table on the next page.

5. Repeat Steps 2, 3, and 4 with the other colors of paper.

GO ON TO THE NEXT PAGE ➤

Name _____   Date _____

What Happens When Light Hits an Opaque Object?, p. 2

Color Reflection

Color of Paper	Color of Reflection
Red	
Green	
Blue	

Answer the questions.

1. What is white light? _____

   _____

2. What color was reflected onto the white paper from each of the three
   sheets of colored paper? _____

   _____

3. What happened to the other colors that make up the white light of the
   flashlight? _____

   _____

4. What happens to light when it hits an opaque object?

   _____

   _____

Unit 2: Let It Shine!

© Steck-Vaughn Company

Physical Science 4, SV 3763-1

Blue Skies, Orange Sunsets

Sunlight is white light. It is made up of all the colors of the rainbow. So, why does the sky look blue? Why does the setting Sun look orange?

✔ **You will need:**

| jar | water | fat-free milk |
| flashlight | partner | |

1. Fill the jar with water. Darken the room. Have a partner shine the flashlight through the water. Look at the light coming into the water. What color is the light?

   _____

2. Stir a few drops of milk into the water. Stand on the opposite side of the jar from the flashlight. Look directly at the beam of light as it goes through the water. What color is the light?

   _____

3. Look at the jar from the side. What color is the light coming through the water?

   _____

When you look through the water and see orange, the blue light is not reaching your eyes. It is bouncing off the milk particles away from your eyes. You can see the blue color when you look at the beam of light from the side.

GO ON TO THE NEXT PAGE ▶

Blue Skies, Orange Sunsets, p. 2

The sky is blue for the same reason. When you look at the sky, you are looking at air full of water droplets and bits of dust. The air is like the milky water in the jar. The dust and water scatter the colors in the Sun's light. Blue light is scattered more than the other colors. It bounces to your eyes from all parts of the sky and makes the sky look blue. When you look at the Sun, you see the yellow that has not been scattered but travels straight to Earth from the Sun.

At sunset, the Sun is low in the sky. Its light goes through more bits of dust and drops of water. Even more of the blue and violet light gets scattered. This leaves more red and yellow to make colorful sunsets.

Answer the questions.

1. Where does the orange light come from? _____

   _____

2. Where does the blue light come from? _____

   _____

3. From the Moon, the sky looks black. Why?
   (hint: There is no air on the Moon.) _____

   _____

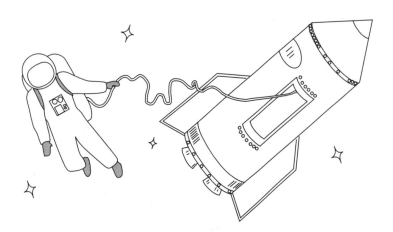

Paints and Dyes

Many of the colors we see around us every day come from paints and dyes. Chemicals and minerals are mixed together to make thousands of different colors. Colors from paints and dyes can be mixed together to give new colors. Blue paint and yellow paint mixed together give a green color. Red and yellow mixed together give an orange color.

Try the following experiment to see what colors make up black ink.

 You will need:

a jar 10 to 15 cm tall	paper towels	water
black marking pen	ruler	scissors

1. Cut a piece of paper towel 2 cm wide and long enough to fold over the top of the jar.

2. Pour water into the jar to a depth of 1 cm.

3. Two centimeters from one end of the strip of paper towel, make a dot of color with a black marking pen.

4. Put the strip of paper into the jar with the color end down. Lower the paper until it touches the bottom of the jar.

5. Fold the top edge of the paper strip over the jar's edge. Do not disturb the paper or jar for one hour.

 Answer the questions.

1. What happened to the black colored dot? _____

_____

2. What colors do you see now? _____

_____

3. What mixture of colors makes up the black ink? _____

_____

Name _____   Date _____

Seeing Colors

You can make a color wheel to learn more about how we see color.

 You will need:

9-cm cardboard circle	1.5 m (5 ft.) of string
red, green, and blue crayons	hole punch

1. Divide the circle into three equal sections as shown in the drawing.

2. Using the crayons, color one section red, the second blue, and the third green.

3. Punch two small holes in the wheel about 3 mm (0.1 in.) on each side of the center. See the drawing.

4. Pass the string through two holes as shown. Tie the ends.

5. Turn the wheel to twist the string. You can now spin the wheel by pulling the string in and out. (This may take some practice.)

Answer the questions.

1. What happens to the colors as the wheel spins?

_____

2. What color do you see?

_____

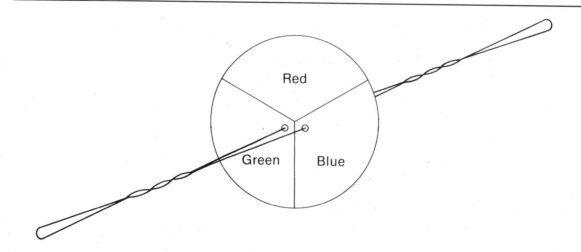

Unit 2: Let It Shine!
Physical Science 4, SV 3763-1

Using Lasers

A laser produces a very narrow beam of intense light. When you shine a flashlight across a room, the beam has spread out by the time it reaches the wall. If you direct a laser across a room, its beam will be the same size on the wall as it was at the source. The energy in a laser beam can be used to cut through metal. A laser beam has many other uses, too.

Some lasers are entertaining, like the spectacular sight of a laser light show. If you watched a light show that used ordinary light, it might not be very exciting. By the time the light got to the sky, it would be so spread out that you would not be able to see it. Because a laser beam is so concentrated, however, you can see it far up in the sky.

Laser beams help doctors perform many operations. For example, before laser surgery was developed, doctors had to use knives to cut into the eyeball to repair damage. Now, laser beams allow doctors to direct a tiny beam of light that can heal the damage without cutting the rest of the eye. Some dentists use a laser instead of a drill to remove tooth decay.

You may have a compact disc (CD) player at home. If you do, you own a laser. In a CD player, the laser beam reflects off the shiny disc. The reflection is turned into a signal that becomes sound when it goes through the speakers. Videodiscs also use lasers. With videodiscs, though, the signals are also converted into a picture that appears on a TV screen.

Many supermarkets now have lasers at checkout counters to read the prices on items. The laser beam moves over the bar code (the block of thin black lines, or bars) on packages. It reads those bars and up pops the price.

 Answer the questions.

1. How is the beam from a laser different from a flashlight beam?

_____

_____

2. Why would someone who runs a store want to use a laser to record the prices of items when a customer checks out? _____

_____

_____

Unit 2 Science Fair Ideas

A science fair project can help you to understand the world around you. Choose a topic that interests you. Then use the scientific method to develop your project. Here's an example:

1. **Problem:** How does the eye work?

2. **Hypothesis:** A model of the eye can help you see how the eye works.

3. **Experimentation:** Make a scale model. Materials: Styrofoam ball or clay, plastic knife, art supplies

4. **Observation:** A model of the eye, showing all parts, helps explain how the parts work together to give sight.

5. **Conclusion:** A model is a hands-on way to learn how the eye works.

6. **Comparison:** The conclusion and the hypothesis agree.

7. **Presentation:** Label all the parts of the eye on the model and prepare a presentation or a report to explain your results. Display your model and report.

8. **Resources:** Tell the books you used to find how the eye parts look and work. Tell who helped you to get the materials and set up the experiment.

Other Project Ideas

1. Some light bulbs are clear, while others are frosted. Why might the frosted bulbs be better to use? Research to find how the white coating on the inside of a bulb affects the light produced.

2. Cameras use lenses to help make pictures. Make a pinhole camera to find out how lenses are used in cameras.

Unit 3 A Simple Force

INTRODUCTION

Students in the fourth grade have a basic understanding of force and motion. They can observe a variety of actions and reactions, and identify how they relate to machines. This unit will give information on force and friction. It will also explain the six kinds of simple machines—levers, pulleys, inclined planes, screws, wedges, and wheels and axles.

FORCES

A force is simply a push or a pull. Forces can be balanced or unbalanced, and it is the interactions of these kinds of forces that create motion. If forces are balanced, there is no movement. For example: if a kite is not moving while you are flying it, the force of the wind is balancing the weight of the kite and the pull of the string. However, if the wind stops blowing, the weight of the kite and the pull of the string would be greater, causing the forces to become unbalanced. The kite would then move.

Forces also differ in size and direction. To move a book, it takes a small amount of force; but to move a bookshelf, it would take much more force. Forces can also come from up, down, left, and right. A force can be measured. Sometimes it is hard for students to understand that when pushing or pulling an object, even though the object does not move, the push or pull can be measured.

Force is measured in newtons. They can be added and subtracted. If forces are going in the same direction, they are added. For example, if someone is pushing a wagon and another person is pulling a wagon, the amount of forces being exerted can be added together. However, if people are pulling in opposite directions, say in a tug-of-war, the forces would be subtracted. The team having the greater number of newtons would have a greater force and would win.

MOTION

The motion of an object is the result when a variety of forces interacts. A change in motion occurs if a still object moves, or if an object already in motion changes speed or direction. Two different forces, acting in opposite directions, will interact so that an object will not move. These forces are considered balanced forces. An unbalanced force results when a force is placed on an object either at rest or in motion, making the object change its state. The object will move faster as the forces become more unbalanced.

Suppose a soccer ball is on the field. It is in a state of rest; the forces are balanced. But if someone kicks the ball, the force of the kick makes the ball move. The greater the force, the faster the ball will go, and the farther it will go. But there is more to motion than just force. The movement of an object is also affected by friction, the force that resists movement.

Friction

Friction is a force that keeps resting objects from moving and tends to slow motion when one object rubs against another object. Every motion is affected by friction. It is useful when movement needs to be slowed, but it causes problems when something needs to be moved. An object's surface determines the amount of friction. Rough surfaces, like concrete, dirt, and grass create more friction. It is helpful when walking, so that people can walk without sliding. These surfaces create a problem when trying to move something over them. Smooth surfaces, like ice and lacquered wood, have less friction, so motion would be easier. Moreover, heat is produced as the objects rub across each other. Early humans used the force of friction to make fire when they rubbed two sticks together.

Mass and surface areas of objects affect the amount of friction. The heavier an object is, the greater the amount of friction. By lightening the load, friction will be decreased, and the load can be moved easily with less force. Similarly, when large surface areas come into contact during motion, friction is greater. By reducing the contact of the surface areas, the object can be moved more easily.

Friction is a factor in a machine's movement, because this force works against the motion of the machine. The machine slows down as the parts rub against each other. In a bike, the rubber of the brakes rubs on the rim of the metal wheel to slow the bike down. In most cases, friction can be reduced by using lubricants, materials like oil or soap. Lubricants coat the surface of an object to decrease rubbing. Machines need lubricants to reduce the friction when parts rub against each other. This helps to keep the parts cool to avoid fire hazards as well as to keep them moving smoothly.

MACHINES

Machines are devices that help make work easier. They usually change the amount or direction of forces needed to get a job done by lifting, pulling, pushing, or carrying. Friction usually affects the efficiency of a machine, because the amount of effort is decreased. Some machines are able to decrease the friction, and thus increase the ease of work. There are six kinds of simple machines: levers, pulleys, inclined planes, wedges, screws, and wheels and axles. When one or more of these are joined in one machine, it is a compound machine. The end result is that less force is needed to work.

Simple Machines

A simple machine has no moving parts or only a few moving parts. Simple machines are made with materials close at hand.

Levers

A lever is a bar or board that rests on a point, called a *fulcrum*. If you push down on one end of the bar, the other end rises. The direction of force is changed. By using a lever, you can lift heavy objects, because less force is needed.

Most levers place the fulcrum in the center. The load and the force are at each end. This is known as a first-class lever. When levers are used to lift loads, the force is always applied down. Moreover, the closer the fulcrum is to the load, the easier the work is, generally. A seesaw is an example of a first-class lever. A second-class lever places the fulcrum on one end, the load in the middle, and the force at the other end. The force in this kind of lever pulls up. A nutcracker is a second-class lever. A third-class lever has the fulcrum and load on each end, and the force is applied in the middle. A pair of tweezers is an example of this kind of lever.

Most commonly recognized levers are first-class levers. Ones that fourth-graders will recognize are bottle openers, pliers, crowbars, and spatulas.

Pulleys

A pulley is a wheel with a rope wrapped around it. The wheel generally has a groove in it to keep the rope from slipping off. It is also a kind of lever used to lift heavy things. One end of the rope is tied to the object, and the other end is pulled by a person or machine. The wheel turns freely, so there is little friction with the rope. Using several pulleys in one machine uses less effort to lift something.

There are two kinds of pulleys: fixed and movable. A fixed pulley stays in place as the load is lifted. When pulling on the end of the rope, the direction of the force is changed. The work is easier because the direction of the force is changed. Flagpoles, window blinds, and sailboats use fixed pulleys. In movable pulleys, the pulley is attached to the load, leaving it free to move with the load. A movable pulley is lifted. It makes work easier because less force is needed. Cranes often use movable pulleys.

Inclined Planes

An inclined plane is a flat surface that slopes. Even though the distance to move an object is greater, less work is required to move an object up an inclined plane than to lift it. A ramp is the most common kind of inclined plane. The angle of the plane also affects the force needed to move an object up a ramp. The steeper the plane, the more force is needed to move an object.

Friction is a force that can affect the ease of using an inclined plane. Flat objects being pushed or pulled up an inclined plane would be harder to move up the slope. More force would be needed to move them. Decreasing the surface area of the object or changing the surface area of the ramp would make the work easier.

Wedges

A wedge is a kind of inclined plane. It is made when two inclined planes are joined together to form one sharp edge. Wedges are often used to break something into two parts. The force is applied at the point, giving a greater force to make the work easier. A thinner wedge will not need as much force as one that is larger. Axes, forks, knives, and needles are examples of wedges.

Screws

A screw is an inclined plane that wraps around a rod to make a spiral. The edge of the screw is known as the thread. The thread moves between the wood to break it apart as the screw is turned. Like other inclined planes, screws decrease the amount of force needed to work, but increase the distance needed to move. The closer the threads are, the greater the distance the screw moves. Screws often are used to fasten things together, make holes, or lift objects. Other examples of screws are the stem of a car jack, power drills, pencil sharpeners, and spiral staircases.

Wheels and Axles

A wheel and axle is another kind of lever. It uses a handle to turn around the rod, a fulcrum. When the wheel turns, the rod turns; and when the rod turns, the wheel turns. The axle usually goes through the center of the rod. When the axle is turned, speed and distance are increased, but more force is needed. By turning the wheel, more force is gained, but the speed and distance are decreased. Moreover, the larger the wheel, the more it will need to be turned to complete the job. In this case, less force is needed. Examples of axles and wheels include door knobs, screwdrivers, fishing reels, and pencil sharpeners.

Gears are often used in a wheel and axle system. The wheels are notched with "teeth." Usually two or more gears work together in a machine. Gears connected by a chain, such as in a bicycle, move in the same direction. Gears in which the teeth dovetail, move in opposite directions. Moreover, one gear is often bigger than the others. Even though the distance the large gear travels is greater, causing more effort, the speed of the smaller wheel increases. The speed is determined by the number of notches in a gear. The ratio of large to small notches is often proportional. For example, a large gear may have 20 notches, and a smaller gear will have 10 notches. For each time the large gear turns, the smaller will move twice as fast.

Name _____ Date _____

What Is Work?

A force is a push or pull on something. Work is done only when a force moves an object.

Look at the pictures. In which of the pictures is work being done? Explain your answer.

1.

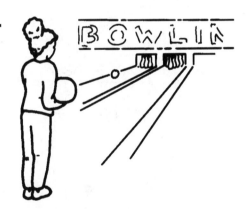

_____

_____

_____

_____

_____

2.

_____

_____

_____

_____

_____

3.

_____

_____

_____

_____

_____

How Do You Measure Force?

A spring scale measures force. When force is measured, you are actually measuring the weight of an object. Each object pulls on the spring with a force. The heavier the object, or the more force an object pulls with, the more the spring scale will stretch. Force is measured in the scientific unit of newtons.

✔ **You will need:**

spring scale   3 books of different sizes   string

1. Tie string around the four sides of a book.

2. Lay the scale and book on the floor. Loop the string around the end of the scale.

3. Pull the scale and book straight up. What is the measure of the force?

4. Record the force on the table below.

5. Repeat Steps 1-4 for the remaining books.

Measuring Force

Book	Force (in newtons)
1	
2	
3	

Answer the questions.

1. Which book needed more force to move? How much force was needed?

_____

_____

2. How did this book compare in size to the other books?

_____

Name _____ Date _____

Calculating Force

Forces can make things move and can change the motion of things that are moving. Two or more forces can act at the same time. If the forces act in the same direction, they have greater effect. If they act against each other, they have a lesser effect. Forces can be added and subtracted using the scientific measurement of newtons. Use what you know about forces, addition, and subtraction to answer these questions.

 Answer the questions.

100 newtons
→

75 newtons
→

1. Sarah and David are trying to move a wagon. David is in front of the wagon and is pulling with a force of 75 newtons. Sarah is behind the wagon and is pushing with a force of 100 newtons. What is the total force acting on the wagon? Which way will the wagon move?

    _____

    _____

2. Suppose Sarah starts pulling on the back of the wagon with a force of 100 newtons instead of pushing it. Which way will the wagon move? Why?

    _____

    _____

GO ON TO THE NEXT PAGE ➤

Unit 3: A Simple Force

     Physical Science 4, SV 3763-1

Calculating Force, p. 2

250 newtons ←   260 newtons →

Chris's Team   Emily's Team

3. Some students are having a tug-of-war. Chris's team is pulling with a force of 250 newtons. Emily's team is pulling with a force of 260 newtons. Which way will the rope move?

_____

_____

4. Emily is pulling with a force of 60 newtons. But she slips and lets go of the rope. How much force is her team now pulling with? Which way will the rope move? Explain your answer.

_____

_____

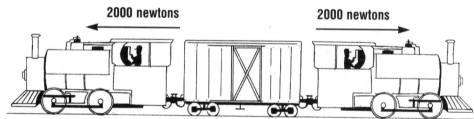

2000 newtons ←   2000 newtons →

5. A locomotive is hooked onto each end of a boxcar. Each locomotive is pulling on the car with a force of 2,000 newtons. Will the boxcar move? Explain your answer.

_____

_____

6. Suppose the locomotive on the left is unhooked from the boxcar. What is the total force on the boxcar now? Which way will the boxcar move?

_____

_____

 Unit 3: A Simple Force
Physical Science 4, SV 3763-1

Machines and Work

There are many simple machines in the picture. Find as many of them as you can and write down their names, what types of machines they are, and how they make work easier.

_____

_____

_____

_____

_____

_____

_____

_____

_____

_____

_____

_____

Name _____   Date _____

Machines at Home

You are learning about simple machines and work.
You can better understand how we use simple
machines in our homes by completing this activity.

Take a simple-machine survey of your home. Find as
many simple machines as you can. List each one you
find in the table below. Tell what kind of simple
machine it is and what work it does.

Simple Machine	Type of Simple Machine	Work It Does

Unit 3: A Simple Force
Physical Science 4, SV 3763-1

Types of Levers

When you see two people on a seesaw, you are watching a first-class lever at work. The fulcrum is in the middle. The person who is closer to the ground is providing the effort. The person in the air is the load that is being lifted.

There are other classes of levers, too. Look at this diagram.

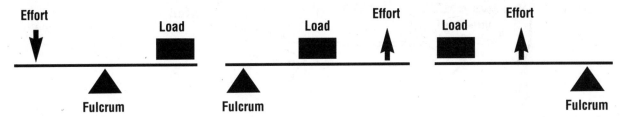

A second-class lever is one in which the load is in the middle, while the effort and fulcrum are at opposite ends. An example of this kind of lever is a bottle opener.

A third-class lever is one in which the effort is in the middle, with the load and the fulcrum at opposite ends. The arm of a person using a tennis racket to hit a ball is an example of a third-class lever. The shoulder is the fulcrum, the arm applies the effort, and the load, or resistance, is the ball hitting the racket.

Answer the questions.

Look at these drawings. Tell which class of lever each is.

1. Pliers

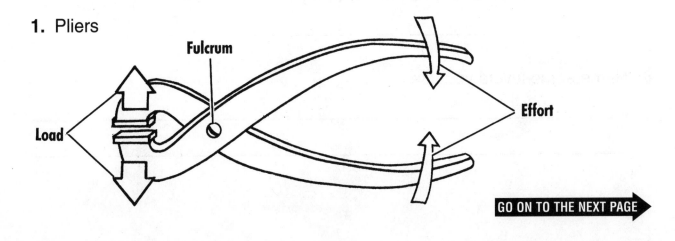

GO ON TO THE NEXT PAGE ▶

Unit 3: A Simple Force

Types of Levers, p. 2

2. Nutcracker

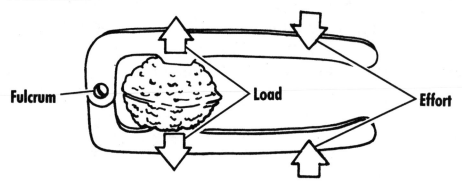

3. Tweezers

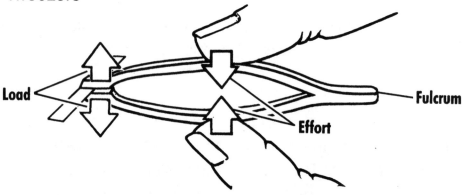

4. Look at the picture of the nutcracker. What will happen if the load force is stronger than the effort force?

_____

5. Which demonstrates a first-class lever, a person using a crowbar to pry a rock out of the ground, or a person using a wheelbarrow?

_____

6. Name some levers you use.

_____

_____

Force and the Fulcrum

A lever is a simple machine made with a board or bar that moves on a fulcrum. The fulcrum is the turning point for a lever. A lever makes work easier because less force is needed to lift or move an object.

✔ **You will need:**
2 small paper cups	wooden ruler, 30 cm long
box of paper clips	marker clay
piece of chalk	tape

1. Label one cup *L* for *Load.* Label the other cup *F* for *Force.*

2. Tape a cup to each end of the ruler.

3. Place a ball of clay on the desk. Press a piece of chalk lengthwise into the clay. It will be the fulcrum for your balance.

4. Put 10 paper clips into the *L* cup. Set the ruler on the fulcrum so that the top edge of the *L* cup is 8 cm from the chalk. Put enough paper clips in cup *F* to balance the load. It will be difficult to balance the load unless you work carefully and slowly.

5. Record your findings on the table on the next page.

6. Remove the paper clips from cup *F*. Repeat Step 4 with cup *L* at 12 cm, at 15 cm, and at 18 cm from the fulcrum. Record your findings.

GO ON TO THE NEXT PAGE ➤

Force and the Fulcrum, p. 2

Fulcrum and Force

Fulcrum at	Force (Number of Paper Clips)
8 cm	
12 cm	
15 cm	
18 cm	

Answer the questions.

1. Did you use more or fewer paper clips as the load got farther from the fulcrum?

   _____

   _____

2. How does the position of the fulcrum affect the amount of force needed to lift a load?

   _____

   _____

   _____

Clever Levers

A lever is a kind of simple machine. A lever multiplies force. Each picture below shows a tool that is a kind of lever. Below each picture, write the name of the tool. Then write what it does. Finally, write *F* on the picture to show where the fulcrum is. Remember that some machines may be two levers sharing one fulcrum.

1.

Tool: _____

What It Does: _____

_____

2.

Tool: _____

What It Does: _____

_____

3.

Tool: _____

What It Does: _____

_____

4.

Tool: _____

What It Does: _____

_____

5.

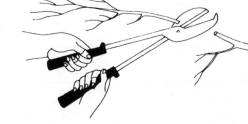

Tool: _____

What It Does: _____

_____

6.

Tool: _____

What It Does: _____

_____

Name _____ Date _____

Look at Levers

1. Which diagram is incorrect? Explain why.

1.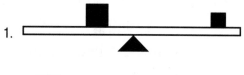

2.

3.

_____

_____

_____

2. Which of these hammers would you use to pull nails out of wood? Explain your choice.

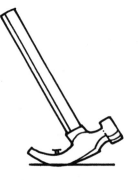 

_____

_____

3. How does a lever make doing work easier? _____

_____

_____

Comparing Forces

It takes force to lift something. The force needed to lift an object is equal to the weight of the object. You can compare the amount of force needed to lift various objects. To do this, you can make a special kind of lever.

> ✔ **You will need:**
> shoe box   quarter   scissors   ruler   penny
> round pencil (or knitting needle)
> long cardboard tube (from paper towel or plastic wrap)
> small objects such as marbles, paper clips, and keys

1. Measure the length of the shoe box. Divide the length by 2 to find the middle of the box. Mark it with your pencil. At the middle, measure 3 cm down from the top of the box. Make a mark, as shown.

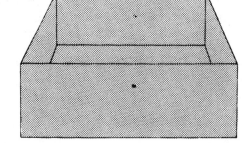

Do the same thing to the opposite side of the shoe box. The marks should be exactly opposite each other.

2. Carefully push a pencil (or knitting needle) all the way through the box at both of these marks. Then take the pencil out and set it aside. Now you have a stand for your lever.

3. Check that the cardboard tube fits lengthwise in the shoe box. If it is too long, cut off enough to make it fit easily.

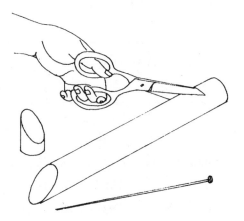

4. Measure the cardboard tube to find the center. At this point, carefully push your pencil through both walls of the tube.

5. Cut off the upper part of each end of the tube as shown. Now you have pans for your lever.

GO ON TO THE NEXT PAGE ➤

Comparing Forces, p. 2

6. Push the pencil through the hole on one side of the shoe box, through the cardboard tube, and through the opposite side of the shoe box. Now you have a lever balance. What is the fulcrum? _____

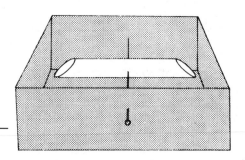

What is the lever? _____

7. Place the quarter in the right-hand pan. What happens to the tube? _____

_____

What force is pushing the right-hand pan down? _____

8. Place a penny in the left-hand pan. What happens to the levels of the two pans?

_____

_____

What causes the change? _____

_____

Which exerts more force—the penny or quarter?

_____

How can you tell? _____

_____

9. Compare the amount of force applied by the different small objects you collected. Then make a list of the objects below. At the top of the list, write the object that exerts the most force. At the bottom, write the object that exerts the least force. Write the rest of the objects in order between these two.

_____

_____

Force and Inclined Planes

An inclined plane is an example of another simple machine. It is a flat surface that is raised at one end. It is often easier to push something up a ramp than it is to lift the object the same distance, because less force is needed.

✔ **You will need:**

board, 1 m long	3 books
spring scale	toy truck

1. Place the end of the board on the edge of one book to form an inclined plane.

2. Use the spring scale to pull the truck up the inclined plane. How much force was needed to move the truck? Record your findings on the table on the next page.

3. Set another book under the board to make the angle of the inclined plane steeper. Repeat Step 2.

4. Set the last book under the board to make the angle of the inclined plane steeper. Repeat Step 2.

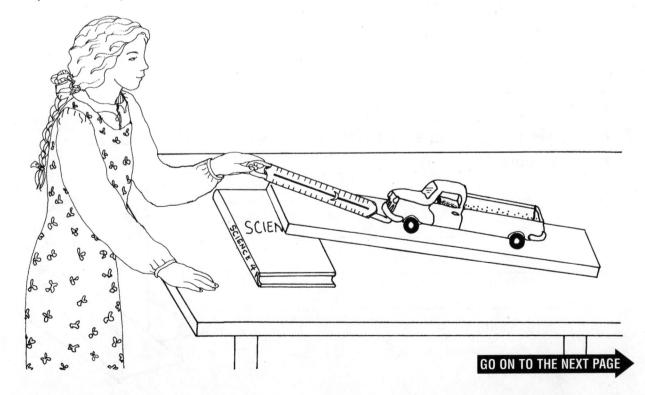

GO ON TO THE NEXT PAGE

Force and Inclined Planes, p. 2

Force on an Inclined Plane

Number of Books	Force

Answer the questions.

1. Which angle required the most force to move the toy truck?

_____

_____

_____

2. Which angle required the least force?

_____

_____

_____

3. How does the angle of an inclined plane affect the force needed to move an object?

_____

_____

_____

_____

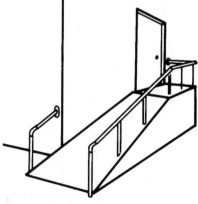

Unit 3: A Simple Force

Ramps

A ramp is an inclined plane. Even though you have to move something farther, less force is needed to move it. Lifting the object straight up requires more force.

1. Which inclined plane will make pushing a box up the ramp easier? Explain.

_____

_____

_____

_____

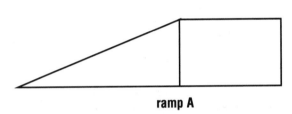

ramp A

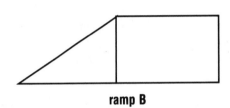

ramp B

2. You need to lift a heavy piece of furniture into the back of the truck. Which of the two boards would you use as an inclined plane to make the job easier? Explain.

_____

_____

_____

Unit 3: A Simple Force

Wedges

A wedge is another kind of simple machine. It is formed when two inclined planes join together to make a sharp edge. The force is focused on this edge, making something move apart.

Look at the pictures. Tell how each tool is an example of a wedge.

1.

_____

_____

_____

_____

_____

2.

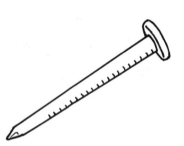

_____

_____

_____

_____

_____

3.

_____

_____

_____

_____

_____

Screws

A screw is another kind of simple machine. It is actually made from an inclined plane and a wedge. The point of the screw is the wedge, because it pushes wood or metal apart. The inclined plane is the part formed by the thread. It wraps around the stem of the screw.

Answer the questions.

1. What simple machine is hidden in these two objects?

_____

   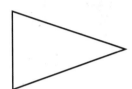

2. Which of the screws shown below would be the easiest to screw into a piece of wood? Explain your answer. _____

_____

_____

_____

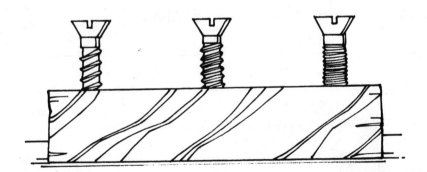

3. In the above pictures, which screw would take the most turns of the screwdriver?

_____

Pulleys

A pulley is made by wrapping a rope around a wheel. The wheel has a track around it to hold the rope in place. A pulley that does not move is called a fixed pulley. It makes work easier because it changes the direction of the force. A pulley on a flagpole is a fixed pulley. A movable pulley is fastened to the load. As the rope moves, the pulley and the load both move. It makes work easier by making the force less.

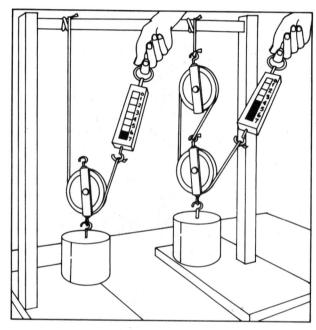

 Answer the questions.

1. Which pulley system above makes work easier? Explain.

_____

_____

_____

2. What other objects use pulleys?

_____

_____

Name _____ Date _____

How Do Pulleys Make Work Easier?

It is easier to pull or push an object than it is to lift it. A pulley changes the direction of the force so that lifting an object is easier.

1. Fill the pail $\frac{1}{4}$ full with sand.

2. Lift the pail with the spring scale. Record the force needed to lift the pail on the table on the next page.

3. Place the meter stick across two desks. Then tie one end of the string to the meter stick. Run the string through the pulley. Tie the free end of the string to the scale.

4. Hook the pail onto the pulley. Pull on the scale to lift the pail. Record the force on the table on the next page.

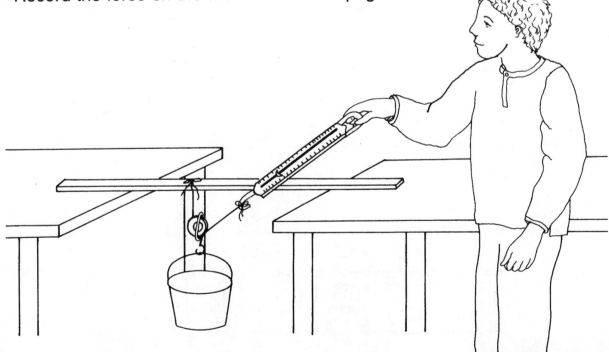

GO ON TO THE NEXT PAGE ➡

Unit 3: A Simple Force

How Do Pulleys Make Work Easier?, p. 2

Force for Lifting Pail

Step	Force
2	
4	

Answer the questions.

1. What kind of pulley system did you use? _____

2. What force was needed to lift the pail in Step 2?

   _____

   _____

3. What force was needed in Step 4?

   _____

   _____

4. How does using a pulley help make lifting an object easier?

   _____

   _____

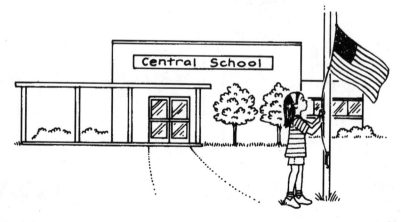

Unit 3: A Simple Force

Physical Science 4, SV 3763-1

How Does a Wheel and Axle Make Work Easier?

A wheel and axle is a kind of simple machine. A wheel turns on a rod when force is applied on the wheel. Even though it takes more hand movement to turn the wheel, less force is needed to do the work. Sometimes it is hard to find the wheel and axle in tools. Some examples are screwdrivers, pencil sharpeners, and fishing reels.

 You will need:
2 screwdrivers, both the same length but with different-sized handles
2 screws, about 2.5 cm long
wood block   hammer   permanent marker

1. Put a mark on each of the screwdriver handles.

2. Lightly tap the screws into the wood to set them.

3. Use the screwdriver with the thinner handle first. Turn the screw into the block. Count how many times the handle turns as you turn the screw into the block. Record the number on the table on the next page.

4. Now use the screwdriver with the thicker handle. Turn the second screw into the block. Count how many times the handle turns as you turn the screw into the block. Record the number on the table on the next page.

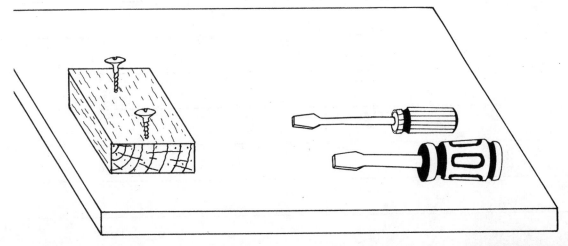

GO ON TO THE NEXT PAGE ▶

Unit 3: A Simple Force

How Does a Wheel and Axle Make Work Easier?, p. 2

Wheel and Axle Turns

Type of Screwdriver	Number of Turns
Thinner Handle	
Thicker Handle	

Answer the questions.

1. In what part was the wheel? _____

2. In what part was the axle? _____

_____

3. Write a paragraph describing the difference between the two screwdrivers. Tell how the difference in their sizes affects the amount of work they can help you do.

_____

_____

_____

_____

_____

_____

_____

_____

_____

_____

How Does a Gear Work?

A gear is a wheel with teeth. Usually several gears work together. When there are large gears and small gears that fit together, they move in opposite directions. The large wheel turns the smaller one. The smaller wheel turns more times and faster than the large gear. An eggbeater is an example of a tool with a small and large gear. Bikes have gears, too. The gears on a bike are connected by a chain. The gears do not touch. They all move in the same direction to make the bike move forward.

✔ **You will need:**

eggbeater   dark crayon

1. Put a mark on one blade of the eggbeater.

2. Slowly turn the large gear wheel of the beater one complete turn. Watch the crayon mark. How many turns did the blade make? Record your findings on the table below.

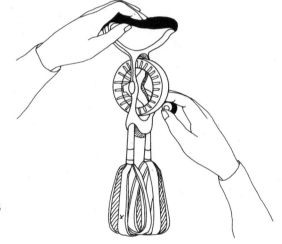

3. Turn the large gear wheel another complete turn. Then repeat a third time. Count the times the crayon mark passes each time. Record your findings on the table below.

Times Blades Turn

Number of Gear Wheel Turns	Number of Blade Turns
1	
2	
3	

GO ON TO THE NEXT PAGE ➤

Unit 3: A Simple Force

Physical Science 4, SV 3763-1

How Does a Gear Work?, p. 2

Answer the questions.

1. How is a gear and wheel system like a wheel and axle system?

   _____

   _____

   _____

2. In an eggbeater, does the blade turn faster or more slowly than the large gear wheel? _____

3. Use the information on the table on page 131 to make a graph of your data.

Unit 3: A Simple Force

Physical Science 4, SV 3763-1

Machines with Wheels

Show the answers on the diagram below.

1. If gear wheel A turns once in the direction shown, how many times and in which direction will gear wheel C turn? _____

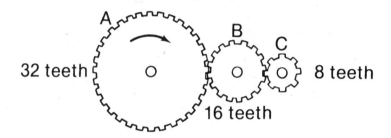

A
32 teeth

B
C
8 teeth

16 teeth

2. If gear wheel A turns in the direction shown in each of the drawings below, in which direction will gear wheel B turn? _____

1   2

A   Bo   A   Bo

3. Gear wheels B and C are joined, so they move together. If gear wheel A turns 10 times in the direction shown, how many times and in which direction will gear wheel D turn? _____

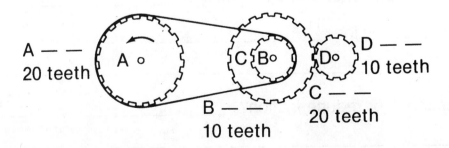

A — —
20 teeth

A o

C Bo

Do
D — —
10 teeth

B — —
10 teeth

C — —
20 teeth

Unit 3: A Simple Force

Physical Science 4, SV 3763-1

Friction and Work

Friction is a force that occurs when one object rubs against another object. It keeps objects from moving. Smooth surfaces cause less friction, and rough surfaces increase friction.

A. If you wanted to move a heavy crate, which method would you use? List the drawings below in order of decreasing friction.

Order:

____

____

____

____

Answer the questions.

B.

1. In which of the drawings above is the most friction present? _____

2. Which drawing shows the least amount of friction? _____

3. Why do wheels reduce friction? _____

_____

4. Why does a polished floor reduce friction? _____

_____

Name _____   Date _____

How Is Friction Affected by Different Surfaces?

Friction is the force that affects the movement of objects. When two objects rub against each other, friction makes it harder to move them. The surface of the objects affects their movement. Smooth, flat surfaces cause less friction. Objects move more easily across each other. Rough, bumpy surfaces cause more friction. Objects with these surfaces are less likely to move.

✔ **You will need:**

small box	sand	string	
spring scale	sandpaper	wax paper	tape

1. Fill the box half full of sand.

2. Tie a string around the box. Then hook the spring scale to the string.

3. Pull the scale to move the box. Record the amount of force needed to move the box on the next page.

4. Put the sandpaper on the table. Tape it to the table. Set the box on it. Pull the box across the sandpaper. Record the amount of force needed to move the box on the next page.

5. Put the wax paper on the table. Set the box on it. Tape it to the table. Pull the box across the wax paper. Record the amount of force needed to move the box on the next page.

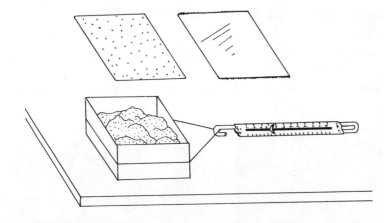

Name _____ Date _____

How Is Friction Affected by Different Surfaces?, p. 2

Surface Friction

Surface	Force
Table	
Sandpaper	
Wax paper	

 Answer the questions.

1. Over which surface was the most force used? Explain.

   _____

   _____

2. On which surface was the friction the least?

   _____

   _____

3. How is friction used on a bike?

   _____

   _____

4. Why do your hands get warm when you rub them together?

   _____

   _____

How Do Wheels Reduce Friction?

Wheels help reduce friction because only a small part of the surface rubs against another object.

✔ **You will need:**

shoe box	4 books	string
spring scale	3 pencils	8 marbles

1. Put all the books in the shoe box.

2. Tie a string around the box. Then hook the spring scale to the string.

3. Pull the box across the table using the spring scale. Record how much force is needed to pull the box on the table on the next page.

4. Put the pencils under the box. Now pull the scale to pull the box across the table. Record how much force is needed to pull the box on the table on the next page.

5. Put the marbles under the box. Space them so they are equally spread under the box. Now pull the scale to pull the box across the table. Record how much force is needed to pull the box on the table on the next page.

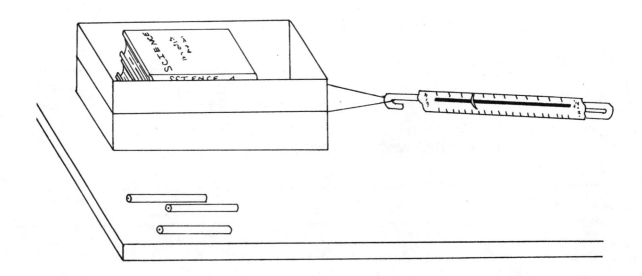

GO ON TO THE NEXT PAGE ▶

Unit 3: A Simple Force

How Do Wheels Reduce Friction?, p. 2

Wheels and Friction

Surface	Force
Table	
Pencils	
Marbles	

Answer the questions.

1. What acts like wheels? Explain. _____

_____

_____

2. In which example was friction the greatest? Explain. _____

_____

_____

3. In which example was friction the least? Explain. _____

_____

_____

4. List some ways you use wheels every day. _____

_____

_____

Do Lubricants Reduce Friction?

In a machine, parts may rub together. A machine is less efficient with friction. A lubricant is a material that helps the parts rub across each other more smoothly. Oil is one kind of lubricant.

✔ **You will need:**
vegetable oil   2 marbles

1. Rub your hands together for about 15 seconds. How do your hands feel?

2. Put a small amount of oil in one of your palms. Rub your hands together again. Now how do your hands feel?

3. Wash your hands. Be sure to wash all the oil off.

4. Rub your hands together while holding the marbles. How do the marbles feel in your hands?

5. Put a small amount of oil on the marbles. Rub your hands together while holding the marbles. How do the marbles feel in your hands now?

GO ON TO THE NEXT PAGE ➤

Unit 3: A Simple Force

Do Lubricants Reduce Friction?, p. 2

Answer the questions.

1. What lubricant did you use? _____

2. How did rubbing your hands together with a lubricant compare to not using a lubricant? _____

_____

_____

_____

3. How did the lubricated marbles feel compared to the marbles that were not lubricated? _____

_____

_____

_____

4. How does a lubricant affect friction?

_____

_____

_____

_____

_____

Unit 3 Science Fair Ideas

A science fair project can help you to understand the world around you. Choose a topic that interests you. Then use the scientific method to develop your project. Here's an example:

1. **Problem:** How are animal and plant body parts like wedges?

2. **Hypothesis:** A wedge is an inclined plane that moves into or under an object. Animals, like woodpeckers, and plants, like a rose, have adaptations like wedges to help them survive.

3. **Experimentation:** Materials: animal and plant pictures, seeds, teeth, or other examples of wedges in animals and plants.

   Collect pictures or physical examples of plants and animals that show wedges. Research how this characteristic is used to help each survive in its environment.

4. **Observation:** Animals have many adaptations that look like wedges, including birds' beaks, animals' claws, and the roots and seeds of plants.

5. **Conclusion:** Pictures and physical examples show the wedge-like adaptations of animals and plants.

6. **Comparison:** The conclusion and the hypothesis agree.

7. **Presentation:** Display the pictures and examples showing wedges in nature. Label each with the animal or plant name, the feature, and its use.

8. **Resources:** Tell the books you used to find background information. Tell who helped you to get the materials and set up the experiment.

Other Project Ideas

1. A hovercraft is a kind of boat, but it does not float in the water. Find out how a hovercraft moves.

2. An elevator is a device that uses a series of pulleys. Research to find out the kinds of pulleys used, and make a model.

Physical Science Grade 4
Answer Key

p. 9 1. F 2. T 3. T 4. T 5. F 6. b. 7. d.
p. 10 8. a. 9. c. 10. b. 11. c. 12. d. 13. a.
p. 11 1. T 2. T 3. F 4. T 5. T 6. b. 7. c.
p. 12 8. b. 9. d. 10. d. 11. a. 12. d.
p. 13 1. T 2. T 3. T 4. F 5. F 6. d. 7. b.
p. 14 8. b. 9. a. 10. c. 11. d. 12. a. 13. a.
p. 19 1.-3., answers will vary.
p. 20 1. c. 2. d. 3. d. 4. The stereo is producing sounds, which travel through the air as vibrations. When the sounds reach the glasses, it makes them vibrate as well.

p. 22 1. When the pot is struck, the sound waves hit the plastic wrap, causing it to vibrate. The rice then begins to vibrate. 2. The rice moved slightly or not at all. 3. The rice moved a lot. 4. Answers will vary. 5. When a sound is made, it moves away in a wave. As the sound wave hits other objects, it causes them to vibrate. The louder the sound, the more an object vibrates.

p. 23 1. guitar strings 2. vocal cords of baby 3. hands 4. hammer and nail 5. saw 6. harp strings 7. wings 8. vocal cords of dog

p. 24 1. The wax paper vibrated. 2. Yes; The stream of air caused the wax paper to vibrate against the comb. This vibration makes a sound we can hear. 3. Yes; The vibration of the wax paper causes it to vibrate against the lips.

p. 25 1. d. 2. Sound travels better through solids than it does through air. Since the door is a solid, you would be able to hear something on the other side if you pressed your ear to it. 3. The person could feel the speaker to know if it was vibrating.

p. 26 1. Solid: You could feel and hear the sound vibrations of the tuning fork more clearly as they traveled through the table. 2. Gas; While you could faintly hear the vibrations as they moved through the air, you could not feel them.

p. 27 1. the metal pot 2. Yes; Sound travels better through a hard solid. Metal is a harder solid than wood. 3. hard objects

p. 28 1. no 2. air 3. water 4. granite 5. 4,999 − 4,877 = 122 meters per second faster 6. 6,096 − 332 = 5,764 meters per second faster

p. 30 1. The ruler moved up and down, causing a humming sound. 2. The sound stopped. 3. The ruler was shorter; the sound was higher. 4. When the ruler was longer, the sound was lower. 5. By changing the size of an object, the sound it makes will change.

p. 32 1. The ends of the straws vibrated when air passed over them. 2. The longer instruments made lower sounds. The shorter instruments made higher sounds. 3. Woodwind instruments make a sound when a reed vibrates. The straws did the same thing. 4. The sound was made when the straw vibrated as the air crossed the reed and also as it moved down the length of the straw. 5. Answers will vary.

p. 34 1. Bottle 6 has the shortest air column. 2. Bottle 1 has the longest air column. 3. Bottle 6 made the highest pitch. 4. Bottle 1 made the lowest pitch. 5. The more air that is in the bottle, the lower the pitch will be.

p. 35 1. 3; Sounds are made when the hand hits the plate, when the pebbles hit themselves, and when the pebbles hit the plate. 2. When the hand strikes the plate, it causes a vibration. This vibration makes the pebbles vibrate against themselves and the plate.

p. 36 1. The wax paper and the paper roll vibrate. 2. To change sounds, you could use a different size roll, loosen or tighten the wax paper, or change the hole size.

p. 37 1. The carton and pencils vibrate. 2. The sound of the drum can be changed by using different sizes of sticks or sticks of different materials. It can also change by using cartons of different sizes.

p. 38 1. The sandpaper vibrates. 2. Answers will vary.

p. 39 1. The ball pushes the first book in each row over. The push is passed on to the next book in each row, causing all the books to fall. 2. Sound waves move out in all directions. As they spread out, they bump into other air molecules and other objects, causing them to move, too.

p. 40 The answers are in the following order: 2, 5, 1, 4, 6, 3.

p. 41 1. b. 2. c. 3. a. 4. d.

p. 42 The answers are in the following order: 4, 1, 5, 2, 3.

p. 43 When you hit the pan, it causes vibrations. These vibrations are sound waves that travel through the air. The sound waves make the plastic vibrate. The sugar then vibrates from the movement of the plastic.

p. 44 1. The stretched plastic is like the surface of the eardrum. It vibrates like the eardrum. 2. Sound waves are vibrations traveling through the air. They cause the eardrum to vibrate, which sends signals to the brain. The brain reads the signals as sounds. 3. Neither the metal pan nor the spoon were touching the plastic, so sound waves must have traveled to the plastic. As they hit the plastic, the sound waves caused the plastic to vibrate. 4. If the sound was loud, the sugar would jump more. If it was soft, the sugar would jump very little.

p. 45 For 1.-3., answers will vary.

p. 46 1. loud 2. loud 3. soft 4. soft 5. loud 6. soft

p. 47 1. jackhammer, gunshots at firing range, explosion

p. 48 2. breathing 3. (talking) 25 decibels − (whispering) 10 decibels = 15 decibels 4. Answers will vary: about 60 decibels 5. noisy home-55 decibels; loud conversation-50 decibels; movie soundtrack-45 decibels 6. Check students' graphs.

p. 50 1. An instrument called an echo sounder sends off sound waves through the water. The waves hit the bottom of the ocean and bounce back to the ship. The time it takes is calculated to find how deep the ocean bottom is. 2. 34 km 3. about 549 meters below the surface 4. about 2,013 meters 5. about 1,464 meters high 6. Possible answer: to find ancient shipwrecks.

p. 52 1. Deaf people can use telephones. They can communicate more quickly and easily than before. 2. A deaf person can call for help. Other people can call to give important information, such as warnings about dangerous storms. 3. Yes; They may need to communicate important information to each other or just wish to chat. 4. Deaf people communicate through mail, computers, and sign language. They get information through lip reading and through closed captions on television.

p. 59 1. light source 2. reflects light 3. light source 4. light source 5. light source 6. reflects light

p. 60 1. Students should say "no," unless there is a lot of dust in the air. 2. The water made the light visible. 3. The light reflects, or bounces off, the water so the eyes can see it.

p. 62 1. Yes 2. The light was blocked 3. Possible answers: There were shadows around the circle of light on the moved card. The first card blocked all the light except where the hole was. 4. Yes; The light was blocked when the middle card was moved. Shadows were formed around the circle of light. 5. It is reflected or absorbed.

p. 64 1. The circle on the paper got wider as the light moved away. 2. The light was less bright as the flashlight moved away. 3. Light spreads out and dims as it moves away from the light source.

p. 65 1. Line should be slightly longer and to the left of the 1:00 line. 2. The 2:00 line should mirror the 10:00 line. 3. The straw blocks the light from the Sun. 4. After recording where the shadow falls at different times throughout the day, you can tell time by the position of the shadow.

p. 66 curtain: translucent; lamp shade: translucent; glasses: transparent; water glass: transparent; book: opaque; window glass: transparent; chair: opaque

p. 67 1. glass 1 2. glasses 2 and 4 3. glass 3

p. 68 1. Students will see a series of images. 2. Answers will vary, depending on the angle. 3. The number of images decreases as the angle gets larger.

p. 69 1. Check students' work. Reflection lines should be at same angle as the incoming light. 2. Check students' work. Reflection lines will be different, depending on the surface each arrow hits.

p. 70 1. Light reflects off the person and travels in a straight line to the periscope. The light enters a hole in the periscope, bounces off the first mirror, and heads straight to the second mirror. The light bounces off the second mirror and travels to the eye. 2. Mirrors reflect the light. 3. twice 4. The mirrors must be at the same angle. If the angle of one mirror changed, the periscope would not work because the angle of the reflection would change.

p. 72 1. Mirror; It has a smooth, shiny surface so the light does not scatter as it reflects. 2. Crumpled foil; While the foil has a shiny surface, it was not even, causing the beams of light to scatter. 3. Mirror; It has a smooth, shiny surface. 4. Smooth foil; While it is not as shiny as the mirror, the smooth surface keeps the light beam from scattering. 5. Answers will vary, but should be materials that have smooth, shiny surfaces.

p. 74 1. The angle of the reflection changed. 2. They are the same. 3. A mirror reflects a beam of light. 4. By changing the angle of the mirror, you can change the angle of the reflected light.

p. 76 1. The candle looks like it is burning in the glass. 2. The glass reflects the light. 3. The glass has a smooth surface. 4. You see the plastic glass and water. 5. The glass is translucent.

p. 80 1. The light became brighter. 2. The light became brighter. 3. The mirrors can be angled so that their reflection hits one spot. 4. Several flat mirrors can be angled so they act like one curved mirror.

p. 81 1. A concave mirror bends in and a convex mirror bends out. 2. The concave mirror is behind the lightbulb. The lightbulb reflects back to the mirror, and the beams bounce out and hit a focus spot which is brighter. 3. The mirror is used for security. Because it gathers a wider range of beams, it can see a wider angle.

p. 82

4. flat: periscope; concave: flashlight; convex: store mirror 5. 2 and 3 6. 3

p. 84 1. The sides of a concave mirror curve inward, and the sides of a convex mirror curve outward. 2. The image is small and right side up. 3. The image is small and upside down. 4. flat; same 5. convex; smaller 6. concave; larger

p. 86 1. The light moves in a straight path. 2. The light beam bends. 3. You can increase the angle of the light. 4. Light travels through air at a different speed than through water. When the reflected light moves from the pencil, the light also changes material. It bends, making the pencil look broken.

p. 87 1. both focus light to a point. 2. Lenses enlarge or reduce the sizes of objects we can see. 3. Light enters one side of the lens and bends as it moves from air to glass. As the beam exits the glass, it bends a second time as it hits the air. 4. Possible answers: telescope, microscope, eyeglasses, magnifying glass.

p. 88 A. Check students' work. B. 1. magnifying glass 2. eyeglasses 3. camera 4. microscope 5. telescope

p. 90 1. Light beams reflect from an object to a person's eye. The light passes through the cornea and the lens. These parts bend the light beams together, focusing them on the retina. The image of the object forms on the retina. 2. Light is focused in front of the retina in nearsighted people. Light is focused behind the retina in farsighted people. 3. The shape changes where the light is focused.

p. 92 1. The light bends as it enters the prism, separating the colors in light. The colors are bent again as they exit the prism, spreading out more. 2. A spectrum is seven colors that make up light. 3. Water, like glass, can bend light. A raindrop bends rays of sunlight and produces a spectrum of colors. 4. Sunlight hits a raindrop and bends several times, making the spectrum of colors in the rainbow.

p. 94 1. The water bends the light. 2. The mirror reflects the light so we can see it. 3. red, orange, yellow, green, blue, violet (indigo), purple (violet) 4. No; The makeup of white light stays the same.

p. 96 1. White light is clear light made up of seven colors. 2. The color reflected was the color of the paper being tested. 3. The other colors were absorbed by the paper. 4. The color of the object is reflected to our eyes so we can see it. The other colors are absorbed.

p. 98 1. It comes from white light from the flashlight. 2. It comes from white light from the flashlight. 3. Since there is no air, there is no water or dust in the sky. Therefore, there are no particles to spread the light in different directions.

p. 99 1. The colors spread away from it. 2. Answers will vary. Likely colors are purple, red, and blue. 3. Answers will vary. Likely colors are purple, red, and blue.

p. 100 1. They blend together. 2. white

p. 101 1. A laser beam is concentrated along its length. A flashlight beam spreads out. 2. The laser would be more accurate than entering in the prices, and it would speed up the checkout process.

p. 107 1. Yes; The boy is moving a wagon by pulling it. 2. No; The girl is standing still and holding a bowling ball. 3. Yes; The girl is moving snow by pushing a shovel.

p. 108 Answers will vary.

p. 109 1. The total force is 100 newtons + 75 newtons = 175 newtons. The wagon will move forward. 2. The wagon will move backward, because Sarah is applying a greater force than David is.

p. 110 3. The rope will move toward Emily's team. 4. 260 newtons – 60 newtons = 200 newtons; The rope will move toward Chris's side, because his team is pulling with greater force. 5. The boxcar will not move, because the two forces are equal, or balanced. 6. The total force on the boxcar is 2,000 newtons. The boxcar will move to the right.

p. 111 ax: a wedge that chops wood; hammer: a lever that pulls nails; seesaw: a lever that moves up and down; screw: a screw holds things together; shovel: a lever that dips; balance: a lever that finds weight; wheelbarrow: a lever that moves things; ramp: an inclined plane that helps things to rise; screwdriver, a wedge that turns screws.

p. 112 Answers will vary.

p. 113 1. first-class lever

p. 114 2. second-class lever 3. third-class lever 4. The nut will not crack open. 5. The crowbar is the first class lever. 6. Answers will vary. Possible answers include bottle opener, poptop of can, pronged end of hammer.

p. 116 1. more 2. The closer the fulcrum is to the load, the less force is needed to lift the load.

p. 117 1. nutcracker; cracks open nuts 2. can opener; opens lids on cans 3. shovel; helps to dig dirt 4. hammer; pounds in and pulls out nails 5. pruning shears; cuts through tree branches 6. screwdriver; turns screws and pries open lids.

p. 118 1. 2; To balance the seesaw, the larger person needs to be closer to the fulcrum and the smaller person needs to be at the end of the seesaw. 2. hammer with longer handle; A lever with a longer handle requires less force to work. 3. A lever can move objects. Less force is needed to move the object.

p. 120 6. pencil-fulcrum; tube-lever 7. The right pan sinks and the left pan rises because the force of the quarter is pushing it down. 8. The left pan sinks slightly and the right pan rises because of the downward force of the penny. The quarter; The pan

with the quarter in it is still lower than the one with the penny. 9. Answers will vary.

p. 122 1. The angle made using 3 books. 2. The angle made using 1 book. 3. The steeper the angle of an inclined plane, the greater the force needed to move an object up the incline.

p. 123 1. A; The angle of the inclined plane is lower. It will take less force to push it up a long, gentle slope than the short, steep slope of ramp B. 2. 1; Board 1 is longer, so the angle of the slope will be less. Thus, it will be easier to move the furniture into the truck.

p. 124 1. ax; separates wood 2. nail; separates wood 3. plow; separates soil

p. 125 1. inclined plane 2. The screw with the most threads will be easier to turn into the wood because the angle of each inclined plane is less than in the other two screws. 3. The screw with the most threads.

p. 126 1. The picture with the two pulleys makes work easier. It uses both a fixed pulley and a movable pulley. The direction of force is changed and less force is needed to raise an object. 2. Possible answers: flagpoles, sailboats, cranes.

p. 128 1. movable pulley 2.-3. Answers will vary, but should be expressed in newtons. 4. It is easier to push or pull an object than to lift it straight up. A pulley can be used so that an object is lifted by being pushed or pulled.

p.130 1. handle of screw driver 2. metal stem of screwdriver 3. The screwdriver with the thinner handle is harder to turn; although fewer turns are used to complete the job. The wheel is smaller, so more force is needed to turn the screw in. With the thicker handle, more turns are needed to embed the screw, but it is not as hard to turn. So, the thicker handle sacrifices the distance the hand turns, but less force is required to complete the job.

p. 132 1. Both use a wheel and axle, but in the gear system, the wheel has teeth and there are generally two or more gears together. 2. The blade turns faster than the large gear. 3. Check students' work.

p. 133 1. clockwise 4 times 2. example 1-clockwise; example 2-clockwise 3. counter clockwise 40 times

p. 134 A. 2, 4, 3, 1 B. 1. 2 2. 1 3. Only a small part touches the ground at one time. 4. The surface of the floor is smoother.

p. 136 1. sandpaper; The surface is bumpy and rough. 2. wax paper; The surface is smooth and flat. 3. The rubber pads of the brakes rub on the rim of the tire, causing friction. The bike slows and stops. 4. Rubbing causes friction and friction causes heat.

p. 138 1. The pencils and marbles act like wheels. 2. The box without pencils or marbles caused the most friction, because the total surface bottom of the box rubbed against the table. 3. The marbles caused the least friction because their surface touched the box and table the least. 4. Answers will vary.

p. 140 1. vegetable oil 2. There was less heat with the lubricant, and the hands felt slippery. 3. The marbles produced less heat and were more slippery. 4. A lubricant reduces friction by creating a slippery material between two materials.